Shop Soiled ~~£7.45~~

£3.95

GW00739330

H₂

Room for Improvement

KITCHENS

KITCHENS

Roma Jay and Phyllis Oberman

W. Foulsham & Co. Ltd.

London · New York · Toronto · Cape Town · Sydney

W. Foulsham & Company Limited
Yeovil Road, Slough, Berkshire, SL1 4JH

ISBN 0-572-01269-1

Copyright © 1984 W. Foulsham & Co. Ltd.

Photoset in Great Britain by Input Typesetting Ltd,
London, SW19 8DR and printed in Hong Kong

Acknowledgements

Special thanks go to the following manufacturers
who took photographs specially for the book.

Aga-Rayburn, Glynwed Appliances, PO Box 30,
Ketley, Telford TF1 1BR.

Robert Bosch Limited, PO Box 166, Rhodes Way,
Watford, Herts WD2 4LB.

Corian – Du Pont (UK) Limited, Richmond House,
16 Blenheim Terrace, Leeds LS2 9HN.

Leisure Sinks, Meadow Lane, Long Eaton, Notts
NG 10 2AT.

Mobalpa (UK) Limited, Unit E Griffin Industrial
Park, Stephenson Road, Totton, Southampton
SO4.

Teisseire Cuisines, Kitchen Design & Advice, 254
Watford Way, London NW4 4UJ.

Thanks also to these manufacturers who supplied
photographs for the book.

Grovewood Products Limited, Concord Lighting
Limited, Dulux Paints – ICI Paints Division,
Beekay Kitchen Furniture Limited, Allmilmo
Limited, Neff (UK) Limited, Colston Domestic
Appliances Limited, Royal Doulton, Barking –
Grohe Limited, Belling & Company Limited,
Cannon Industries Limited.

Special thanks also go to the following people.

Vivienne Charrett who enlightened us on the
technicalities of lighting.
Tracy Cohen for transforming scrappy drawings into
neat plans.
Cynthia Freedman who translated illegible writing
into neatly-typed manuscripts.
Jeanine Laine who interpreted difficult ideas into
visual drawings.
Tony Timmington who patiently and expertly
clicked the camera.

Contents

Chapter 1

Introduction

The expenditure on a modern fitted kitchen is often the second biggest household expense after actually buying a house. The average housewife is often totally bewildered by the plethora of kitchen units and equipment screaming at her from the lavishly illustrated books and magazine advertisements that abound. Pictures of dream kitchens suggest how simple it is to be transported into an environment which makes life easier. But it is not that easy to achieve. Buying and installing a new kitchen is traumatic, and even with expert professional help, can be a long, painful process!

Kitchen planning is seen by many consumers as a mystery, to say nothing of the effort of hacking through the jungle of units and appliances! Many people therefore, just hand over the whole job to a kitchen studio, shop or even a doorstep salesman whom they are obliged to trust to do an expert job on their particular kitchen. But without a real understanding of your needs and your lifestyle, no one can design a kitchen that is exactly right for you - it may look beautiful, but will it work for you and your family?

This book attempts to present what is practical and possible by relating directly to real people's lives, helping you to analyse your specific needs and become aware of all the complexities involved in fitting a new kitchen. We discuss the basic principles of the 'work triangle' - from storage to preparation to cooking - another way of expressing time and motion study. We also cover safety and hygiene; the importance of structure itself - walls, doors and windows being in the most convenient positions. Plumbing and electrical wiring must be correctly located. Effective ventilation, lighting and colour are vital and without them no one can function at their best. And, of course, there's the question of choosing what equipment is right for you - not merely the most profitable for the salesman to sell!

In preparation for this book we conducted a survey of hundreds of households who had recently installed a new kitchen as well as many whose kitchens had evolved, and we asked them about every aspect of the kitchen, its equipment and how it functioned for them.

The results were a revelation! People who had the same model of cooker, for example, felt totally differently about it. Some loved their latest electronic built-in oven, whilst others found it too complicated. Some found their fridge/freezer large enough, whilst others thought it woefully inadequate. Some thought their twin-bowl stainless steel sinks marvellous, others criticised their stainability and size.

This divergence of opinion also relates to

◊ *A kitchen must suit your particular needs, not the manufacturer's. If you have a chef in the family, you will need plenty of workspace.*

kitchen layouts. What will suit one family will not necessarily suit their next-door neighbours. Someone else's dream kitchen could easily be your nightmare.

This all underlines the essential fact that kitchens should reflect people's lifestyles and be capable of adaptation to changes in those lifestyles. Because change inevitably comes along. Children grow up. Families split up. An elderly parent may come to live. A grown-up child may bring their own family to live within your home.

Our mode of living has changed so much over the past twenty years and continues to do so. We live surrounded by the trappings of a high-tech society. Technology allows man to travel to the moon and back, yet Britain still has around four million homes in serious need of basic improvements. Micro-technology, computers, all the spin-offs of the space programme, video and cable TV all impinge on the way we live both inside and outside our homes.

Other factors which must be considered include rapid world-wide communications, not to speak of the increasing intermingling of races and culture in society, the extension of adult education, and the growing possibility of male-female role reversal at home. Increased leisure time can mean growing fruit and vegetables leading to more creative cooking and preserving, wine making and brewing.

The development of the convenience and packaged food industry and the parallel growth in ownership of freezers has also affected our cooking habits. In some respects people are turning back into the home for their leisure with the ever-escalating costs of entertainment outside. So there is a need for the high technology available to be used to make the kitchen a better and more workable place to use, rather than high-tech as a bolt-on goody – all digital clocks and flashing lights.

This book provides not only a lot of the answers for those who want to make improvements or have a new kitchen, but also states the questions which should be asked at the outset. Don't expect the experts to know what is right for you. The experts should know what can and cannot be achieved technically, but only you know how you live.

High expenses may not, in fact, be involved. A kitchen can often be transformed with a few small but very significant alterations. The position of a refrigerator, the way space is utilised inside existing cupboards, all help to increase efficiency without spending much money. Space can be gained by just changing the way a door opens, or doing away with the door altogether! It is important to discard any fixed ideas about the positions of things in the kitchen – the sink does not have to be under the window, the washing machine does not need to be in the kitchen at all! Making the most of the space available to suit your needs is what an efficient kitchen is about – budget-priced or luxury.

Think hard about the things in your existing kitchen that you really dislike or find impossible to live with. List out every inconvenient item so you are sure to avoid them next time. A good, workable result can be achieved as long as you understand your own real needs and how they have changed since you started using the kitchen, before committing yourself to any financial outlay.

Finance is obviously a critical issue when revamping or replacing your kitchen. Though actual costs are quite difficult for the average householder to estimate accurately, it is vital to decide at the outset how much you are prepared to spend, though inevitably there will always be unforseen extras. This book also outlines the major sources of finance for home improvements such as kitchens.

Chapter 2
The Basic Principles

Efficiency

Kitchen manufacturers' sales literature too often disregards all planning and safety standards. Glossy, full colour pictures show a huge, sunny kitchen, with children playing happily, a smiling, young, attractive 'mum', masses of units, and an island or peninsular unit with saucepans bubbling away merrily on the hob. The reality, however, is much more likely to be a small room with too many doors, and a harassed mother trying to keep her children under control whilst at the same time trying to cook.

Though the vast majority of kitchens are small, manufacturers insist on photographing unrealistically large rooms. How much more sensible to show a small, practical and appealing kitchen. Some of the features they show are far from sensible and can even be dangerous – like an island hob which, unless specifically designed, should be avoided to cut down the risk of fire and protruding saucepan handles. Huge picture windows are often more of a nuisance than an advantage. In summer, the kitchen may get too hot, and in winter large expanses of glass, even when double-glazed, allow easier access for cold from outside.

Safety, efficiency and economy of movement are the keys to good kitchen planning. A basic understanding of these principles at the outset will save both money and tempers. The general aim should be to reduce to the minimum the amount of walking required between the sink, cooker and refrigerator.

The Department of the Environment recommends an ideal 'work triangle'. This ideal area would have sides of not less than 3600 mm and not more than 6600 mm. Within this area all necessary equipment can be placed allowing for safety, economy and efficiency. They also recommend there should be no doors within the 'work triangle'. This cannot always be avoided, but under no circumstances should a door cross the route from the cooker to the sink!

They recommend that 'preparation, dish-

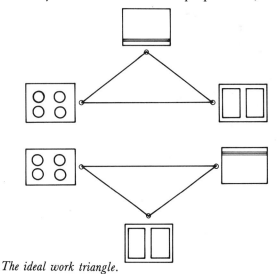

The ideal work triangle.

9

washing and cooking zones should be part of the same continuous run of fitments. Provided they are within easy reach of sink and cooker and are complete in themselves, the zones for food storage and mixing may be separate'.

This, then, is the theory of the 'work triangle', but if this was put into practice the ideal kitchen would be circular! As the diagram shows, the perfect kitchen also has no doors. Obviously, in most situations, it would be impossible to dispense with one door, let alone more than one. But the 'work triangle' can be put into practice, and these examples – illustrating real kitchens not just kitchen plans – show how the basic principles are applied to everyday, and often awkward-shaped kitchens.

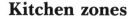

◊ *The working kitchen involves six main elements, and the best layout is circular!*

Kitchen zones

To gain maximum benefit from an existing or new kitchen, the space should be divided into zones, which ideally should not overlap. The three main zones are – Utility – Eating – Working.

Utility

This equipment probably comprises the central-heating boiler, washing machine, dryer, broom cupboard and possibly a sink. The boiler can often be wall-mounted, with the washing machine, dryer and broom cupboard underneath or alongside. Sometimes it is possible to house all or some of this equipment elsewhere in the house, such as a utility room or a bathroom.

Eating

There should be an eating area in every kitchen, whether it is one stool and a pull-out worktop just large enough to take a cup of coffee, or a full-size dining table and chairs. This will, of course, be governed by the size of the kitchen itself, the family and their ages, and how the kitchen is used.

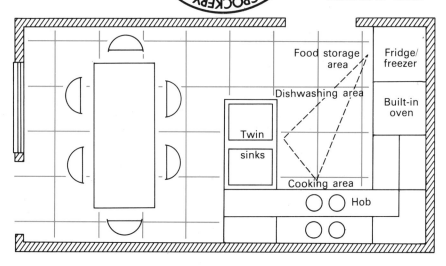

◊ *Most people do not have an 'ideal' kitchen shape with which to work, and this layout shows how the work triangle can be put into practice.*

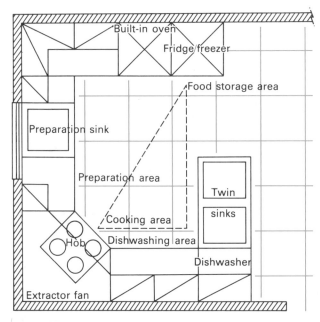

○ ○ *These kitchens illustrate some of the many ways in which the work triangle can be made to work in practice.*

○ *Low-voltage eyeball lights provide a tight, narrow beam.*

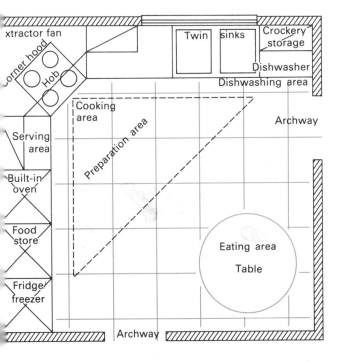

Working

The working zone is further divided into six sections:

1. Storage of food
2. Preparation
3. Cooking
4. Serving
5. Dishwashing
6. Storage of crockery

Kitchen zones in practice

These examples will show you some different ways in which efficient planning of kitchen zones can be put into practice.

This L-shaped kitchen (left) illustrates the way the work triangle of sink/cooker/refrigerator has been adapted to the needs of the family as well as

11

the constraints of the room itself. The workflow sequence is not perfect, but it does make sense. Perfection would have demanded costly major structural work not essential to safety and efficiency.

The U-shaped kitchen/living room (below) illustrates the way in which the utility, eating and working kitchen areas have been created. Within the working kitchen are the six zones: food storage, preparation, cooking, serving, dishwashing, crockery storage. In this case, as the fridge is close to both the working kitchen and the eating area, the food store is not in the ideal position. However, the needs of the whole family have to be balanced against the needs of the cook, and this is an acceptable compromise.

The third example (below right) also demonstrates the way in which the three main areas are constructed. The utility area comprises the boiler and washing machine with brooms placed in an alcove. A breakfast bar running along the back of the peninsular unit creates an eating area. The work triangle is clearly defined.

Safety

It's generally acknowledged that the kitchen is the most hazardous place in the house, so achiev-

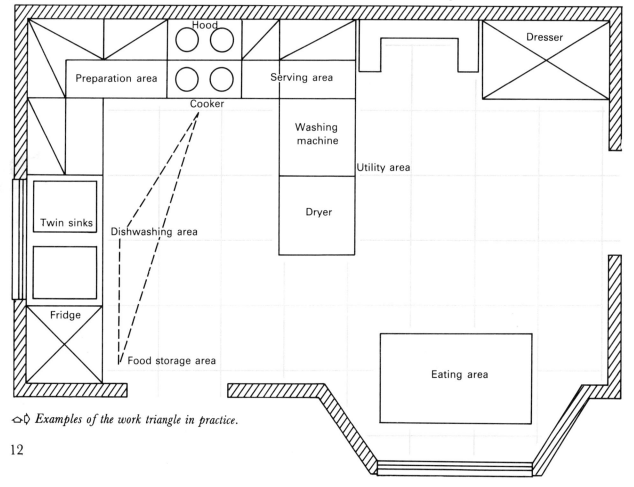

Examples of the work triangle in practice.

ing a safe kitchen is of paramount importance. Major hazards include the positioning of cookers opposite sinks or next to doors; wall cupboards hung too low; slippery or uneven floors; protruding handles and poor lighting. Potentially dangerous substances such as bleach, must be stored at a high level or locked away.

Here are a range of hazards, their effects and the suggested solutions.

Incorrect electrical wiring or insufficient sockets

This can lead to overloading of the electrical circuit and possibly even a fire. Multi-plug adaptors can easily loosen in their sockets leading to overheating and burning in the flexes.

In any working kitchen we recommend the installation of two separate circuits. These should be put in by a National Inspection Council approved contractor (NICIEC – see glossary) and approved by the Electricity Board. One circuit should be a 30–amp ring circuit with outlets for fixed appliances, such as dishwashers, and sufficient sockets for each small appliance such as a percolator or toaster with at least two spare for more rarely-used items. The second circuit should be a 45–amp or 60–amp circuit for the cooker if electricity is used for cooking.

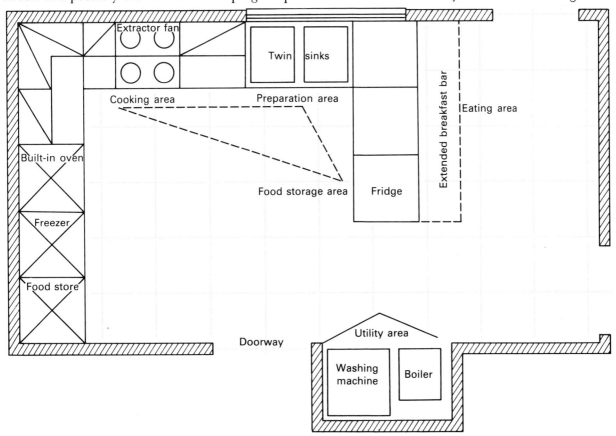

Sockets or switches within reach of water

Shocks or electrocution could result if the wiring is faulty. Sockets and switches should always be well out of the range of accidental splashing and should never be touched with wet hands.

Poor lighting

Eye strain is an obvious result of poor lighting, but less apparent is the hazard of poor hygiene in ill-lit areas. All light fittings should be earthed and professional advice sought about this. Overall lighting should be supplemented by striplights fixed under wall cupboards to illuminate work surfaces and cooking areas.

Water pipe unearthed

If the water pipes are not earthed, leakages could cause shocks when sinks, taps or faulty metallic appliances are touched. All water pipes should be cross bonded using safety earth clamps and earth wires. Seek professional advice either from your local Electricity Board or an NICEIC contractor.

Bad positioning of cooker

A cooker or hotplate by a door, at the end or a run of units, or on a narrow peninsular or island unit is a potential hazard. In these positions, the hotplates or burners and the pan handles are too exposed and unprotected by worktops. Traffic of people in and out of the kitchen could lead to accidents.

The cooker should be adjacent or at right angles to the sink, with a worktop each side of the hob linking it to the sink for easy access.

Sink and cooker on opposite walls

There is a danger of spilling boiling liquids when removing pans off the hob to drain. The sink and hob should be positioned within two metres of each other and linked with a worktop.

The cooker should ideally be next to the sink and linked by worktops for easy access.

Wall units or cooker hood placed too low over cooker and base units

Heat generated by the cooker can distort wall cupboards hung too low. If a pan catches fire, flames will spread more easily to low-hung cupboards. Nasty knocks to forehead or eyes could result when leaning forward. The minimum recommended wall space between the bottom of wall units and the cooker hob is 750 mm. To be safer, fix them at least 900 mm above the work surface.

Sharp or squared off corners and edges on worktops

Adults can sustain bruises, grazes or scrapes and small children more serious knocks to the heads and eyes from sharp corners. Laminated worktops can be obtained ready-made with smoothly rounded edges. Always ask for radius edges or post-formed worktops.

Unhygienic work surfaces

Hazards of food poisoning can be reduced by thoroughly scrubbing any wooden or tiled work surfaces after each use. Danger can lurk in the grouting. Likewise, joins in laminated worktops must be butted up tightly and evenly to minimise places where bacteria can accumulate.

Slippery or uneven floors or differing floor levels

Falls, broken limbs, scalds or concussion can occur from these hazards. Kitchen floors should never be polished to produce a slippery surface. Wet floors should always be dry before use again. When a floor is being laid or renewed, the sub-floor should be well prepared, damp-proofed, ventilated and screeded. Differing floor levels should ideally be covered with material of a different colour, and be well lit at night.

Kitchen step stools should be well maintained and used rarely. If they are in constant use, consider rearranging cupboard contents to make things more accessible.

Flammable wall and ceiling coverings in danger areas

Rapid spread of fire is facilitated by flammable materials on walls or ceilings if a pan of fat catches alight.

These dangers are reduced with the introduction of thermostatically-controlled deep fat fryers, and thermostatically-controlled gas hobs or electric hotplates. A frying pan should never be left unattended unless the fryer, gas or electric hotplate is SWITCHED OFF.

Ceilings should never be covered with expanded polystyrene tiles unless they are of the fire retardant quality. Similarly walls behind the cooker should not be covered with cork or wood unless it is treated with a fire retardant. The kitchen should be equipped with a fire blanket.

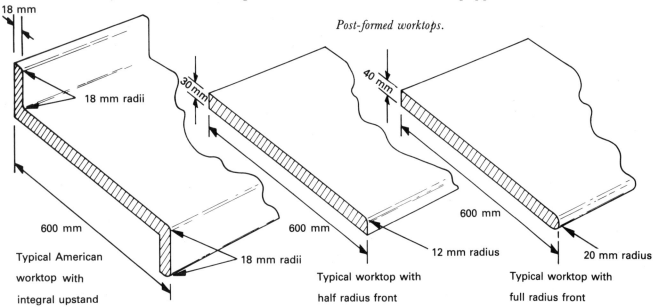

Post-formed worktops.

18 mm

18 mm radii

30 mm

40 mm

600 mm

600 mm

600 mm

Typical American worktop with integral upstand

18 mm radii

12 mm radius

20 mm radius

Typical worktop with half radius front

Typical worktop with full radius front

15

Careless storage of dangerous cleaning fluids or medicines

All dangerous materials should be stored out of the reach of children to avoid accidents or poisoning. Labels should be accurate and lids tightly fixed. To help children treat dangerous substances with respect, the dangers should be taught from an early age.

Storage of sharp knives

Knives kept in crowded drawers leads to cut fingers and blunted blades. A magnetic wall rack should be fitted or knife slot cut into the rear of the work surface.

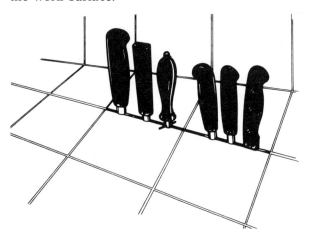

Internal glass doors

Cuts and more severe accidents can occur if the glass is broken, and in case of fire the glass could crack. Conventional solid doors should be used, or specially toughened or laminated glass.

Draughts

Draughts can cause gas flames to blow out (though all modern approved equipment is fitted with flame failure devices). They can make doors slam on fingers or blow pieces of paper onto the cooker hob causing a fire. The draught then fans the flames further. Cooker, doors and windows should be sensibly sited in relation to each other so that a draught is not created.

Poor ventilation

Poor ventilation can lead to a stuffy and drowsy atmosphere and to excessive condensation. An extractor fan placed in the wall above the cooker will help eliminate this problem. If a false ceiling is fitted in the kitchen, this should not be fixed too low.

Rustic or moulded style cupboard doors

Crevices on cupboard doors provide the perfect place for dust, grease and germs. All mouldings, knobs, lattices and hinges should be well-cleaned weekly.

Lighting

Lighting a kitchen is not easy. Most people get it wrong because they don't really understand what the different types of lighting will do for them and how to use lighting to achieve maximum benefit. Subtle yet effective illumination is a skill that few have mastered, yet its importance cannot be underestimated. Too many and too bright lights can cause tension, just as dim lighting causes accidents around the house.

This is an attempt to simplify the complexities and try to illustrate the best lighting for each area.

Simple, direct and bright illumination is required for food preparation, cooking and washing up. This can be provided by a number of different fittings depending on your kitchen layout.

If the working areas have wall cupboards fixed above them, then tungsten striplights or fluor-

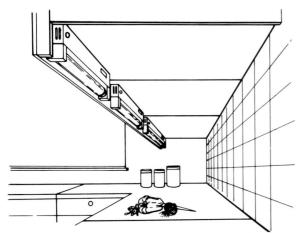

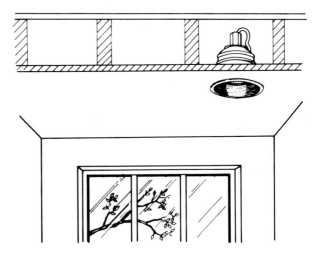

Striplights and recessed downlighters.

escent tubes can be fitted to the underside of the wall units to shine directly onto the work surfaces. Our survey showed that this was the most effective and practical for safety's sake. However the cooker hob should never have a wall unit directly above it. If your hob doesn't have a hood and light over it, a pendant light fitting with an ordinary household (GLS) lamp, or the new 2D lamp directed onto the centre of the area will shed sufficient light. This applies similarly if the sink is sited under a window.

When the eating area is an integral part of the kitchen, softer mood lighting is preferable. This then also provides extra lighting on dull days. Attractive pendants with GLS or 2D lamps can certainly enhance the decor and the choice of available fittings is vast.

Illumination in the utility area must be bright enough to see stains on clothing, read care labels and spot the creases during ironing. If you have a separate utility room a centrally fixed fluorescent tube should meet these requirements.

Besides these basic necessities lighting can be used to create moods. For instance a dropped ceiling with recessed downlighters gives a luxurious feel to a room, but may not be powerful

enough for all your lighting needs. They have to be fitted into a space of 160 mm above the ceiling. If your ceiling height is higher than 2.4 metres, this will not be as effective for working lighting, but simply for overall illumination. According to our survey some householders felt that recessed downlighters were attractive but difficult to unscrew when replacing lamps.

Similarly we found that spotlights were considered most unsuitable as overall lighting. They dazzled, made the kitchen too hot, had very short lives and were difficult to replace. However they are most effective when directed onto a focal point like a picture, chimney breast or curtains at the window. They also produce a diffused beam when pointed towards the ceiling.

If the wall units do not reach up to the ceiling, striplights or fluorescent tubes can be fixed on top of the units in front of plants and small objects to throw attractive patterns onto the ceiling and make a very decorative feature.

Lighting should be planned when you are planning the total kitchen. Before the wiring is done you must ensure the correct positioning of lights and switches. When your kitchen layout is drawn, mark on the plan the location of

17

◊ *Pendant lights are particularly useful and attractive when positioned above a table. The height can be adjusted on many lights.*

◠*Recessed downlights give a luxurious feel, and can be used to highlight surfaces when good illumination is needed.*

◊*Recessed eyeball lights in the ceiling give good overall light, while striplights under the wall units provide extra illumination for working. Pendants are used for decor in the eating area.*

◊ *Striplights can be used both above and below wall units; above, to highlight objects such as plants, below, to give extra light on work surfaces. Spotlights can be directed at specific objects where extra light is required.*

striplights under wall units, utility and dining lighting with switches by their doors, if located out of the kitchen, or by the kitchen door if they are an integral part of the kitchen.

Overall and decorative lighting should have separate switches by the hall/kitchen door.

The lighting plan should really be discussed with a qualified electrician before work is estimated in case he has any recommendations to make.

Types of lighting

The types of lighting can be confusing so here is a brief guide to help your understanding of the subject.

The GLS is the most common. It is cheap, small, neat and easy to replace. Its life expectancy is 1000 hours. It gives out more heat than other types which can present a problem in a small kitchen. More power is used to produce light than by any other type of lamp. Cheap imported GLS lamps have been known to explode, may become detached from their caps or have a cap live to the touch. Only buy lamps which conform to British or European standards. The long-life GLS lamp should last 2000 hours, but at the expense of light output which is considerably reduced.

Tungsten striplights are available in lengths of 221 mm or 284 mm long. Ideal for fixing under wall cupboards, they do, however, get very hot and should never be installed too close to water where they might get splashed and explode. Relatively cheap compared with fluorescent tubes, the life expectancy of a tungsten strip is much less.

Fluorescent tubes have been maligned for being clinical and cold looking. But they do come in warm white colours. They are higher priced than lamps but are efficient and long lasting, giving between 5000 and 10,000 hours of light before gradually diminishing. The colour does affect the look of food, and some tubes give a faithful colour reproduction as well as appearing warm. Ensure your tubes are kept clean as dirt cuts the light output – especially after two years of grime.

A new generation of lamps is emerging which combines the qualities of the fluorescent with the convenience of filament lamps. A neat small, curled up tube, it fits into compact and unusual fittings and is made by leading manufacturers.

Always ensure the power of the lamp suits the fitting. A lamp of too high a wattage could cause a fire hazard from overheated wiring, or the lamp cap sticking in the socket causing the glass to shatter when removing it. Reliably made fittings will specify the maximum power and the most suitable lamp.

Analyse your requirements

Before foraying into the market place to order your kitchen, it is essential to know your needs to plan the layout. Self knowledge can save wasting time, effort and money. Here are some basic questions to help assess your needs.

* How many people are in the household? ....
....

* What are their ages and sex? ....
....

* Is there a place outside the kitchen for your boiler and laundry equipment? ....
....

* Do you need to eat meals, snacks or breakfast in the kitchen? ....-
....
....

* How much cooking do you do? ....
....
....

* Does the cook go out to work? ....
....

* How many people use the kitchen? ....

* Do you grow your own vegetables for freezing or preserving?...

* Do you buy fresh produce for freezing? ....

* Do you brew your own beer or make wine? ...
....

* How often do you cook for visitors? ....
....

* Which units and appliances do you want to retain?..

* Is there any particular feature you wish to incorporate?..
....

* Does anyone in the household have a physical handicap?...
....

* What is it about your existing kitchen that you dislike? ....
....
....

* What structural alterations will improve the layout of the room? ....-
....
....

* What is your budget? ....
....

* Do you intend to move within five years? ......
....

These are basic questions and you may have others to add to the list. The answers help you sort out your priorities. For instance, if your budget is £2000 and you plan to move within five years, there is no point in spending the total on structural alterations. You want the benefit of the new kitchen now. However, if you plan to stay in the house, £2000 invested in knocking down internal cupboards, repositioning doors, windows and so on will immediately improve the room layout. In subsequent years you can add units as more funds become available.

These basic questions will lead towards the achievement of a kitchen matching your lifestyle. For example, the amount of entertaining you do will govern your sizes of cooker and refrigerator. If you do not do much home baking or oven cookery, there's no case for an extra-large oven.

Chapter 3

Utility Rooms

Washing machines have certainly removed the drudgery from washday, but one should have no delusions that even the most sophisticated machines have removed all the work.

The fully-automatic, electronic or computerised job certainly washes better. It copes with delicate and sensitive fabrics and, in many cases, removes stains.

What the machine cannot do is sort the washing into compatible types. It cannot read care labels or washing instructions. It still has to be loaded and unloaded. If a tumble dryer is incorporated into the one machine, some of the load may still have to be put on one side for the dryer to do its job most economically.

After drying, either in the integral tumble dryer, separate dryer or out in the garden, the ironing has to be done and the finished laundry sorted for storing in airing cupboard, drawers or wardrobes.

◊ *This attractive utility and sewing room is light and spacious, and avoids wasting valuable space in the kitchen for washing facilities.*

◊ *To separate laundry equipment from the main part of the kitchen, it can be tucked away under a worktop facing away from the kitchen area.*

◊ *Satin-finish pine doors make this alcove into a useful linen cupboard which also hides the washing machine and tumble dryer.*

sorted for storing in airing cupboard, drawers or wardrobes.

Sometimes garments or linens are badly stained and need pre-soaking, and whilst some of the most recent washing machines have this facility, others do not, so attention is needed before the washing machine is used. Bacteria in soiled clothing means laundry should never be washed in the same sink in which the family crockery has been washed. Gardening clothes, sports gear and boots are not pleasant when removed from sweaty bodies and should, ideally, be kept elsewhere than the linen basket in the bathroom.

Food freezers need air space around them to run most efficiently. If opened and closed too frequently during the day – a temptation when they are located in the kitchen – running costs soar, especially in warmer kitchen temperatures.

Central-heating boilers, so often found in the kitchen, need never be installed there. Lack of imagination on the part of the architect or central-heating engineer is usually the cause.

All this essential household equipment takes up valuable space in the kitchen – space which should be devoted to food and utensil storage, preparation and cooking. In many overseas countries, where space is at a premium – Israel is a typical example – a separate utility room is standard in the home. Yet in Britain this facility is still considered a luxury.

Every house needs a room for sorting, soaking, washing, drying, ironing, to say nothing of the central-heating equipment and the freezer. A utility room is also ideal for gardening clothes and boots, sports kit, raincoats and umbrellas, spare vases and indoor plant containers. How convenient, also, for the service engineer who doesn't intrude in the kitchen, should any of this equipment need attention. Isn't it high time that British developers, architects and builders looked

more closely at the consumer's real needs and designed and built accordingly?

A utility room need not be confined to those highly-priced luxury homes, but can easily be accommodated for the first-time buyer, or in a middle-priced new home with tiny kitchen and bathroom but with generously designed lounge and dining room. It has little to do with additional costs, either. At the design and construction stage it costs no more to relocate internal walls so they allow for a utility room. If a young mother has nowhere to dry nappies and sheets, for example, except in her small kitchen it's

A specially-made cupboard door with storage shelves is easy to construct and convenient.

hardly surprising that her frustration can lead to psychological problems!

If a totally separate utility room is not practicable in your house, look around for alternatives. A cellar or basement could easily be converted to accommodate the utility equipment, as is so common in Canada and the United States. Also consider the garage. Many American homes allow garage space for their laundry equipment. Plumbing and drainage need not be too difficult and electric wiring can always be extended for sockets. With fuel economy extending the trend to smaller cars nowadays, it may well be that the garage could have room for laundry equipment and the central-heating boiler.

The logical place for washing is often the bathroom itself. Dirty laundry frequently starts off in or near the bathroom and finishes there, so why bother to carry it downstairs? It is pleasant to dry the clothes in the garden on a fine day, but that is still possible.

Wiring recommendations for installing a washing machine in a bathroom state that the machine must be permanently wired with neither plug nor socket inside the room. The washing machine must never be sited so it can be touched by someone touching the bath or shower at the same time. (See Chapter 8 for fuller details.)

If none of these options are feasible, a walk-in larder or cupboard could be considered for re-organisation. The cupboard may be in the kitchen or in the hall. If space is tight, a compact central-heating boiler could be fixed on the wall with brooms and cleaning material underneath. Washing machine and tumble dryer can be stacked alongside with useful storage shelves above.

A small but capacious broom cupboard can be devised by fixing terry (or spring) clips and hooks onto battens on the rear wall to take brooms, dusters, brushes, pans, steps and ironing

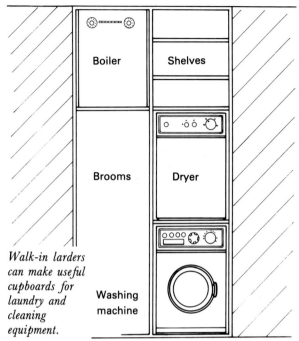

Walk-in larders can make useful cupboards for laundry and cleaning equipment.

board. The inside of the door can be converted to take shelves housing liquids, detergents and cleaning powders. A standard door will not be strong enough to take the weight of packets, drums and containers; the storage shelves should be constructed on a sturdy framework by a competent carpenter or D-I-Yer.

If utility space must be found in the kitchen, then remember that these machines should be separate from the main working area. A peninsular unit which divides the cooking from the eating area could be an ideal home for the washing machine and dryer. Facing away from the kitchen, they need not be obtrusive and could even be hidden behind doors which match the kitchen units.

There may be an alcove or old chimney breast where the laundry machines could be placed and enclosed by louvred doors, thus providing an ideal linen cupboard space.

25

Chapter 4

Eating Areas

When someone is busy cooking in the kitchen, the instinctive urge for visitors or bystanders is to want to have a taste. Eating food where it is prepared is a traditional, and very comforting thing to do. In prehistoric times it was the norm. There was no special room for eating, nor was there co-ordinated linens, crockery and cutlery! Raw materials were simply hunted, harvested or gathered, then roughly skinned, chopped or ground with simple implements. Cooking, where applicable, was over an open fire and eating was a communal process vital to survival.

Historically, cooking and eating habits have refined and continually changed over generations and according to the structure of the social system. Formal dining rooms were associated with privileged sectors of the community – those who had servants to scrub, clean and polish their homes and possessions. The less endowed had no choice but to eat where they cooked. However, for almost all social classes, there was always an occasion when something would be consumed in the kitchen. It was the warmest and cosiest room in the house and was therefore the spot for tea or supper.

The kitchen then needed more elbow grease

◊ Everyone needs space for eating in the kitchen – whether it is a table and chairs or just a breakfast bar. The working and eating areas here are linked by the overall blue theme.

Breakfast bars are particularly useful in small kitchens. This one is suspended by ropes to create an attractive feature as well as extra work space.

and sheer drudgery to clean the fire grates, black-lead the stove and stoke the fires for hot water. In the 1920s, labour-saving kitchens became a fashionable necessity for the liberal middle classes, as servants to perform these menial tasks became less available. The trend-setters felt it was their duty to do most of the cooking, if not the cleaning, themselves, but could not bring themselves to eat in the same room as the one in which they cooked. This explains why, in the period between the two world wars, so many houses were built with such small kitchens in contrast to the proportions of the dining rooms.

Unfortunately, this reactionary thinking still lingers on with many house developers and architects and modern homes are still built without adequate provision for family eating in the kitchen. This is despite the fact that nine out of ten families wish to eat breakfast, snacks or a full meal there – often all three! Family and friends tend to congregate in the kitchen whilst meals are being cooked, and the person cooking likes to be involved in the socialising. This reinforces the belief that the kitchen is still the heart of the home. A place for meals can be provided in many ways, as shown in the following illustrations.

Research has shown that the space needed widthways for a person to sit at a table is 600 mm, including elbow room. Sitting at a table, with legs tucked under it, 400 mm is needed from the table to accommodate the person to sit comfortably, but another 600 mm is required behind the chair for walking, pulling the chair out, and for the action of sitting down. A free-standing table with chairs around it, therefore needs more space in the kitchen than, say, a fixed sit-up bar.

Choosing the location of the eating area requires some radical thinking, overturning traditional views.

A pleasant view of the garden helps make the most mundane meal acceptable. However, all too often the sink is placed under the window. It is assumed – wrongly – that this is the correct and only place for the sink. Another cliché is that people enjoy looking out of the window whilst washing up. Why not so when preparing food, or even eating? When a sink is fixed under a window the space above the sink cannot be used

Flying worktop over base units

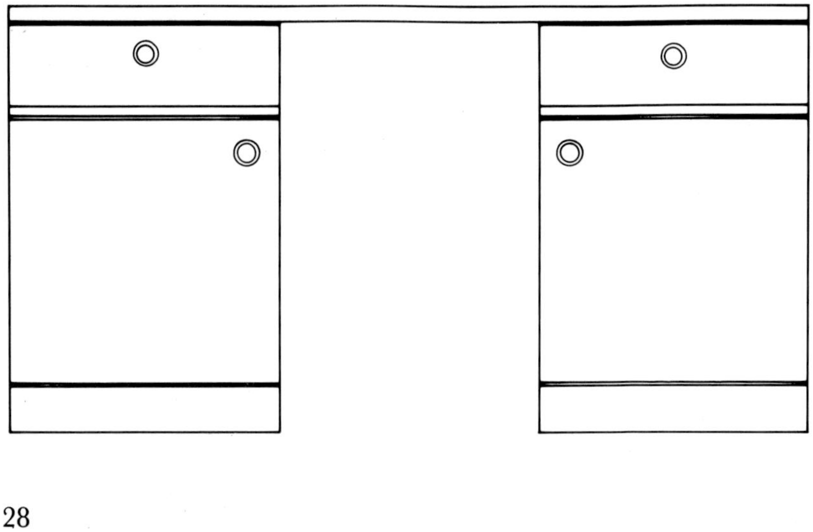

Extended worktop as bar

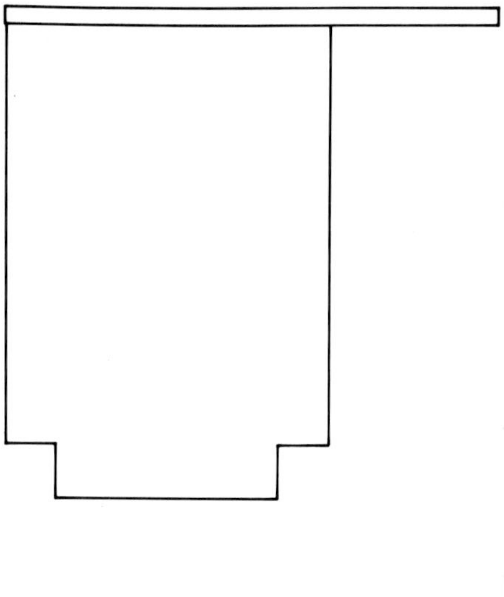

for storage. If the sink is sited against a wall the cupboard above can conveniently hold the crockery, making dishwashing less of a chore. In the kitchen, walls with windows fitted in them are seldom used to the optimum. Siting the eating area here where less storage is required, makes total sense.

Many families demolish the wall between the kitchen and the dining room to create a generous sized everyday living room, and keep another room separate for formal entertaining or peace and quiet.

An L-shaped area between two doors often seems as though it might provide an ideal place for a bench seat and table. However, this may accommodate six or eight people, and if someone in the centre of the bench wishes to leave the table, it can cause a great deal of inconvenience.

A chimney alcove which is not used for storage can often be useful and decorative to house a table and chairs.

A bar attached at the back of a peninsular unit, or a worktop suspended from the ceiling to form a peninsula, makes a good eating area which doubles as an extra work surface when necessary.

For kitchens that are too small for a conventional table or even a bar, the table which pulls out from a unit makes a compact eating area and serves as an auxiliary worktop. Folding chairs can be stored in either a tall cupboard or on hooks on the wall.

Wherever the eating area is placed, be sure there is a unit to store cutlery, crockery, condiments, jams, cereals and other accoutrements nearby. The fridge, too, needs to be between the kitchen and the eating area, so that if drinks or sauces are forgotten, it is not a major trek through the kitchen to retrieve them.

Where space is limited, there are plenty of ways to provide a compact eating area.

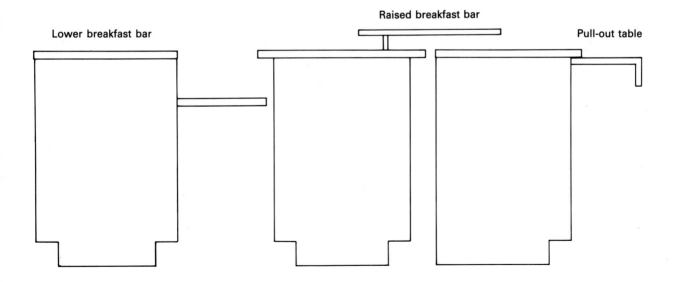

Lower breakfast bar

Raised breakfast bar

Pull-out table

↶ *There is no logical reason to place the sink beneath the window. A pleasant view of the garden from the table brightens up even an ordinary meal.*

◁ *The trend towards a large living area is illustrated here by this dining room and kitchen separated by archways.*

◺ *A good example of space used to suit a particular family, this kitchen is a family relaxing room, with working kitchen, dining and TV areas.*

◁ *A chimney alcove makes an attractive decorative feature in the dining area. (Ideal Home)*

◁◁ *For smaller kitchens, a pull-out worktop is ideal for a handy eating area.*

Chapter 5

The Working Kitchen

The working kitchen divides into six sections:

1. Storage of food
2. Preparation
3. Cooking
4. Serving
5. Dishwashing
6. Storage of crockery.

For efficiency and comfort of operation, it is not only necessary to ensure the layout is right; utensils, gadgets, saucepans – the *batterie de cuisine* – must be in the right places.

Storage of food

Just because the larder has always traditionally held all the food, condiments and spices, there is no reason why things should not be changed around to give greater convenience.

What is the point of crossing to the other side of the kitchen to find the stock cubes or sugar when they are required at the cooker or the table? The larder can then be used for longer-term storage of cans, packets and bottles.

With the growth in ownership of fridges and freezers, the old-style larder is less vital. Some manufacturers have developed chillers within the fridge/freezer cabinet to hold dairy produce and vegetables. Certainly an advance on the traditional larder cabinet offered by most fitted kitchen manufacturers, is the temperature-controlled larder which is cooled but not refrigerated.

Tall, narrow cabinets 300 or 400 mm wide, with pull-out racks attached to the door, make total use of the space and are ideal for small packets and bottles that tend to get lost or fall over on deep shelves.

Preparation

This is the processing of the raw materials – vegetables, fruit, meat or fish. The preparation area should be close to the food store and should include a sink and as large a work surface as possible. There should also be a rubbish bin, waste disposal unit or even a trash compactor. Efficient, and hygienic disposal of waste is not merely a matter of throwing everything into one huge bin! A disposal unit installed into the kitchen sink takes most food scraps. It does not accept cans, bottles, string or paper which must be disposed of elsewhere.

An electrically operated trash compactor, popular in the United States, will neatly compress cans, paper, packages and so on for easy disposal. Keen gardeners may keep a compost heap which will take most vegetable matter, so a separate disposal bag may need to be kept in the kitchen for this purpose. There may be a local bottle bank and waste paper collection, so these items may also be kept separately. To minimise odourous waste, keep only a small bin to be emptied frequently.

Cooking

Cooking areas may be divided into two if there is a split-level cooker. A built-in oven and hob should not be sited too close together as there is little room for preparation of different types of foods ideally suited to split-level cooking.

The hob is used for dishes requiring regular attention. But once in the oven, roasts, cakes, puddings and so on, require little attention until cooked. Saucepans should be stored under the hob. Kitchen tools, condiments and herbs are best in a wall cupboard to one side of the hob.

By siting the oven away from the hob it is easy to store the cake, pastry and bread making equipment, rolling pins and so on where they would be used. The oven housing unit can easily hold ovenware, baking tins and trays, whilst weighing scales, mixer, baking ingredients,

spices and cooking foil can be stored next to it.

However, if the oven and hob are one piece of equipment, either free standing, built-under or slip-in, all the same items need to be stored close by, but on opposite sides to each other. For instance if your saucepans are stored on the left of the cooker, your baking trays and mixer should be stored on the right.

The grill can either be above the hob at eye level, or above, in or under the oven. The ideal height and position depends on the volume of grilling. If you grill a lot, you should ensure the extractor fan is powerful enough to remove the fumes. If the fan is immediately above the grill then there should be no problem. If the grill is in or under the oven and away from the hob and fan, then odours will be slower to extract.

The efficient removal of cooking fumes and

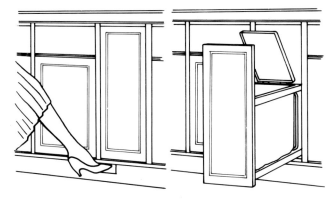

Small waste bins can be hidden in deep drawers. The lid pops up automatically when the drawer is opened.

Hooks inside cupboard doors are a handy way of storing cooking utensils. Condiments should also be stored near the hob.

33

The working kitchen

This unusual circular kitchen illustrates the perfect cooking circle. (Ideal Home)

A well fitted and ventilated larder is a sensible way to store many foods.

This integrated fridge, freezer and cold store is built in to match the kitchen units.

grease is of prime importance. An extractor fan fitted into the wall above the hob will remove steam and fumes. This can only be fitted in an outside facing wall, so the hob should, ideally, be fixed against this wall. If this is impossible, a ducted hood, or a charcoal filter hood above the hob is a partial solution, but they must be cleaned frequently to be efficient. Cooker hoods must be fitted at least 900 mm above the hob to avoid rapid spread of flames in the event of fire. If a bare fan is fitted into the wall above the hob, it can be concealed behind a false, open bottomed wall unit.

Microwave ovens standing free on a worktop clutter up the kitchen, and they should, if possible, be built into the oven housing unit. Some manufacturers match their ovens and microwaves so they can be built into housing units.

This kitchen illustrates a clearly defined work sequence.

Peninsular units are a useful way of dividing the working kitchen from the eating area.

As outlined in Chapter 2 the hob should be linked by a worktop to the sink. It should also have ample work surfaces on both sides of it. Kettle, tea, coffee, cups and saucers are best kept close to the sink. Toasters should be on a work surface or shelf near to the bread. Deep drawers for bread storage are preferable to bins on the work surface.

For regular use, sandwich makers, cling film, foil and plastic bags, plus the bread knife should be conveniently close. The knife can be safely stored in a slot at the back of the work surface.

The kitchen on page 2 is a good example of the preparation and cooking areas, using a built-under oven and hob bisecting the corner and making a compact yet adequate preparation and cooking areas. The rustic style hood conceals an extractor fan and fits in with the kitchen more decoratively than conventional hoods.

Serving

As long as there is sufficient work surface beside the hob, the oven or the free-standing cooker on which to put plates and serving dishes, there should be few problems.

Within the serving area there should be convenient storage for oven gloves, serving spoons, plates and serving dishes.

Dishwashing

This is often a part of the preparation area. However, if the kitchen is large enough, it may be worth considering a separate dishwashing zone, close to the eating area. This is shown in the diagram at the top of page 11. This zone will accommodate the waste disposal unit or a rubbish bin and, ideally, a dishwasher. Twin sinks should be large enough to hold a grill pan or large baking trays. Sinks are available with a variety of accessories including a chopping board, vegetable sieve, draining rack and a separate drainer, all of which fit over either sink. A wall cupboard above the dishwasher is useful for storage of crockery. If you do not have a dishwasher, a drainer cupboard above the sink holds dishes, plates and cutlery and is both labour- and space-saving. This is only feasible if the sink is against a wall rather than a window.

Sink units are not designed with storage facilities for washing up liquid, wire wool, brushes and dishcloths, so ingenuity must be applied to find ways of storing these close to the sink. A rack fixed to the inside of the unit door is practical and some manufacturers do offer these as optional extras. Advanced technology has been brought to the development of ovens and washing machines, but not yet to the problem of storing and using washing-up equipment!

Drainage racks can be hung above wall-facing sinks for convenient crockery storage.

Storage of crockery and cutlery

These should be near both dishwashing and eating zones. Table cutlery should be kept in drawers separately from other kitchen gadgets. Cups can be hung from hooks on the undersides of shelves, inside wall units or in a special china cupboard if there is room for one. Fine china can be stored on the high shelves of wall units if they are not required on a daily basis. Glasses and jugs need to be kept near to the water supply and to drinks in the fridge, hence the recommendation that the fridge be situated between the eating and cooking areas. Plastic lidded containers, so useful for leftovers, should also be kept handy. Items which are less frequently used – large salad bowls, fish kettles, huge stock pots – can be stored in corner cupboards or, again, in high cupboards at the top of appliance housing unit.

The peninsular unit shown in the photographs on page 35 separates the working kitchen from the eating area and houses twin sinks – usable from either side, so the user can face the windows overlooking the front of the house or the French doors to the garden. The dishwasher is fitted beside the sinks and facing into the eating area, so the table can be cleared and the equipment loaded easily.

The work sequence of storage/preparation/cooking/serving is clearly defined in this kitchen so each function has its own space. Work surface right round links up each of the zones. The four-burner gas hob is fitted diagonally across one corner of the kitchen – a very safe location offering more working space around it for utensils and ingredients. Above the hob, an extractor fan is camouflaged by a corner hood tiled to match the walls. The double electric oven is built in with work surface on one side and a built-in fridge/freezer on the other.

Chapter 6

Storage and Ideas
and Simple Solutions

Everyone has their own pet ideas on storing items that no standard kitchen unit could accommodate. For example, units don't provide little hooks for all those rubber bands we can't bear to throw away! So full marks to those British kitchen unit manufacturers who do look beyond merely what their Continental rivals provide, and actually try to see what the housewife really needs.

Recipes and recipe books are never provided for. Recipe cards or small notes are not easy to handle whilst making a new cake for the first time. A bulldog clip and a cup-hook attached to the underside of the wall unit solves this problem. Attach the recipe to the bulldog clip and simply hang it on the hook! Winchmore Kitchens have produced a recipe book holder which looks, when closed, like part of the pelmet concealing the striplight under the wall cupboard. When it is pulled out it holds the book – just like a mini-lectern.

Built-in larders are often valuable space-wasters. Converting one to a compact utility room has been described in Chapter 3. Another practical use is as a telephone booth, holding directories, message pad and a small seat.

Alternatively, it could be equipped as an office by installing a small work surface and chair, plus shelves for recipe books, household accounts and other essential kitchen notes, and a telephone. Line the walls with cork and they become a pinboard for messages – an ideal area away from kitchen clutter to plan menus for the week and work out household budgets.

Hooks are the most useful aids in the kitchen. Attach them to the underside of shelves or wall units to hang cups, jugs, kitchen tools, wooden spoons and so on. Dispensers to hold foil, cling film and paper towels can be fixed to the wall between wall-hung units and the work surfaces.

A knife slot cut into the back of the worktop holds sharp kitchen knives safely. The slot should

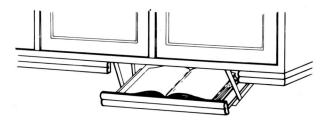
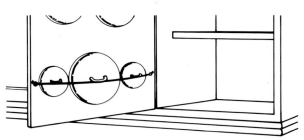

Simple, space-saving storage ideas for wall cupboards.

37

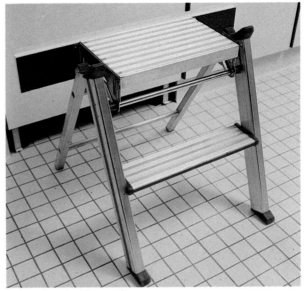

⌂ *Folding steps can easily be stored in the plinth area beneath units.*

◊ *This obsolete larder has been converted into a useful telephone booth.*

◊ *A pigeon-hole wine rack is a sensible use of space above this fridge and microwave.*

✿ *Some like their* batterie de cuisine *to hand, and this iron frame suspended from the ceiling keeps awkward-shaped items tidy and accessible.*

◊ *A slim car radio fixed to the underside of a wall unit avoids the clutter and wasted space of a free-standing radio on the worktop.*

◊ *The ultimate in high-tech, these wire shelves are suspended from walls and ceiling to provide storage space for all kinds of kitchen equipment.*

be just wide enough to take the blades, but too narrow for the handles to slip through.

Saucepan lids clatter around in the cupboards when pans are taken out. A cheap and simple solution is to stretch curtain wire in rows on the inside of the unit door and two or three lids can be securely held by each row. Tupperware make a rack to hold their lids and this, again, can be attached to the inside of a door.

For spice jars and small packets, narrow plastic racks can be bought in hardware stores or household departments and these can be fixed inside cupboard doors for efficient use of space. They should not be overloaded, however, as they could pull the door off its hinges.

Conventional waste bins take up a lot of room, either free-standing or within a cupboard. You can buy a Garbina holder that fits neatly on the inside of the sink unit door and holds bags, either polythene or heavy duty paper. It takes less space and ensures that rubbish does not stay around too long while a larger bin is filled.

A plastic grid, again easily obtainable in household departments, can be attached to unused wall space. Matching hooks can then take all those odd shaped items which belong to no specific category – for example, small watering cans, kitchen aprons and keys.

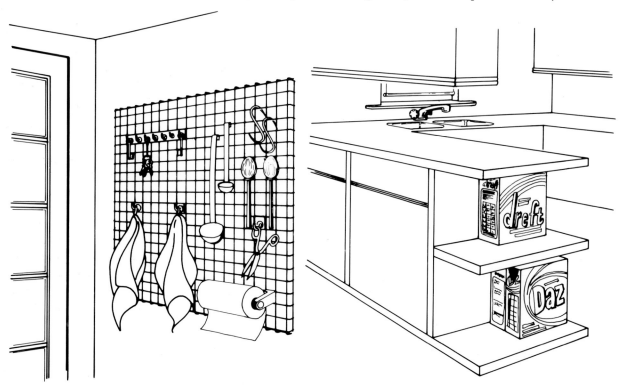

A plastic grid on the wall is ideal for storing awkward-shaped items.

Overhang shelves are a useful idea for the end of a work surface.

At the end of a run of units, or a peninsula, the worktop can overhang to accommodate shallow shelves below for frequently used items such as washing powders.

Plinths below base units can be a great waste of space, but some manufacturers make practical use of the space – folding steps by Bosch are stored in the plinth area and make excellent aid to reaching top cupboards.

Serious wine buffs would never store their wine in the kitchen, but those less committed wine drinkers can accommodate bottle racks; suitable pigeon holes for wine bottles are also found filling spaces between units. In Chapter 7 we show the

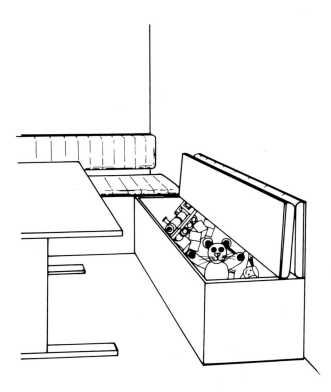

A bench seat with a lift-up top makes a convenient toy box.

space above the built-in fridge and microwave usefully occupied with round bottle holes.

Fresh herbs can be continuously available from a supply of little pots on the window sill. An alternative is a macramé holder suspended from the ceiling, holding a pottery dish with individual herb pots.

A free-standing fridge should not have a unit fixed directly on top of it, so there will often be a space between the top of the fridge and the underside of the wall unit. A slim car radio fixed to the underside of the wall unit is a perfect filler for this space.

A bench seat with a lift up lid is an ideal place for storing toddlers' toys.

Saucepans, sieves, ladles, casseroles, cake racks and many other items in the *batterie de cuisine* can be stored on an iron frame suspended from the ceiling above this island unit. There is less chance of mislaying these things if they are on show.

A novel way of concealing electric wiring, plumbing and uneven walls, without the need to build a false wall, is a worktop and continuous back panel. Made out of one piece of laminate, the angle is post-formed or curved and the back extends up to the underside of the midway wall units.

Finally, the ultimate in hi-tech storage, Ariston of Italy produce a kitchen which seems to have the solution for many 'where-to-put-what' problems. Green shelves are suspended from hooks in the ceiling and walls. Under these, wire racks are attached to hold paper towels, bottles, etc. There is a double basket for cups and glasses, slide-in bulb lights protected by wire, and even a cutlery holder which slopes down when in use then folds back neatly under the shelf. Even the handles on the doors and drawers do double duty as hooks for tea towels, oven gloves, bags and so on. (Photograph page 39.)

Chapter 7

Kitchen Layouts

A square shape is common to probably millions of kitchens. It is typical of the post-war semi-detached, the pre-war detached, or the newly-built house. This shape lends itself to many interpretations and meets the needs of many families, as these following examples show.

A kitchen for a growing family

This young couple have one child and the possibility of more to come. In this first home, with a limited budget, they wished to spend it as wisely as possible. First priority is the working kitchen, which must be efficient, safe and as timeless as possible. They could not afford it to look old fashioned within a few years.

Sensibly, the washing machine and a sink were plumbed in the garage where the central-heating boiler had already been installed to allow more space in the kitchen. The fridge/freezer, fronted by decor panels to match the units, was placed next to the garden door. Adjoining this is the gas double oven. Base and wall units link up to the double-bowl, round red enamel sinks under the window. Continuing round the kitchen, units link up to the matching red gas hob with an extractor fan above. Base units continue from

the hob up to the peninsular breakfast bar – also a useful extra work surface. To make use of the end of the wall unit (see picture left) a midway unit, normally wall mounted between worktop and cupboard above, was fitted to hold cruet, jam, sugar and so on in handy reach of those using the breakfast bar.

As the budget was tight, wall units were fitted at a level to allow another tier up to the ceiling to be added when funds permitted.

◊ A square kitchen can be adapted to suit any needs. This design gives plenty of work surface and a useful breakfast bar for a young family.

A very similar kitchen design, but offering more storage space for a family with older children. (Ideal Home)

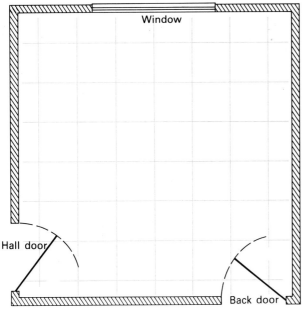

A basic square kitchen can still be quite unique if well designed.

Family with teenagers

The same shape kitchen in a detached house is used by a family with two pre-teenage children. Their needs were similar to the first example, but there was a higher budget available. The growing family also meant a greater need for storage. (Photograph page 43.)

Their solution, in fact, was quite similar. Additional storage was provided by fitting cupboards underneath the breakfast bar and taking the wall units right up to the ceiling. A much-needed dishwasher was included in the layout which proved suitable for several stages in the life of this growing family.

A busy kitchen

The next example is a family with three children aged between 13 and 20, two dogs and numerous

frequent visitors. Their house is large and detached with a morning room between the kitchen and the front of the house. The washing machine and other utility equipment were installed in the garage to free space in the kitchen. (Photograph page 46.)

Whilst they had no need to eat main meals in the working kitchen, they wished to have breakfast and snacks there, while maximising on much-needed storage space. The family decided to make some structural alterations when planning their new kitchen and these gave the room more useable space. The garden door was moved further along the same wall and the door to the morning room was moved to the right which allowed a longer run of units between the two doors. One of these base units holds a pull-out table for snacks.

On the left of the morning room door a tall cupboard holds brooms and folding chairs. Adjacent is a built-in fridge and a built-in gas oven. Base units link up to the window wall where a dishwasher is installed beside the double sink. To the right of the sink a gas hob and grill are fitted with an extractor fan fixed above. Wall and base units complete the layout up to the garden door.

Living room/kitchen

This detached mock Tudor house had three large store cupboards designed as part of the house, but entered from the garden. Probably originally intended for storage of fuel and gardening implements, these store cupboards backed onto the kitchen.

The family with two teenage children desired

♦ Moving a door can create new possibilities. This design for a three-children, two-dog family provides ample storage, work and eating space.

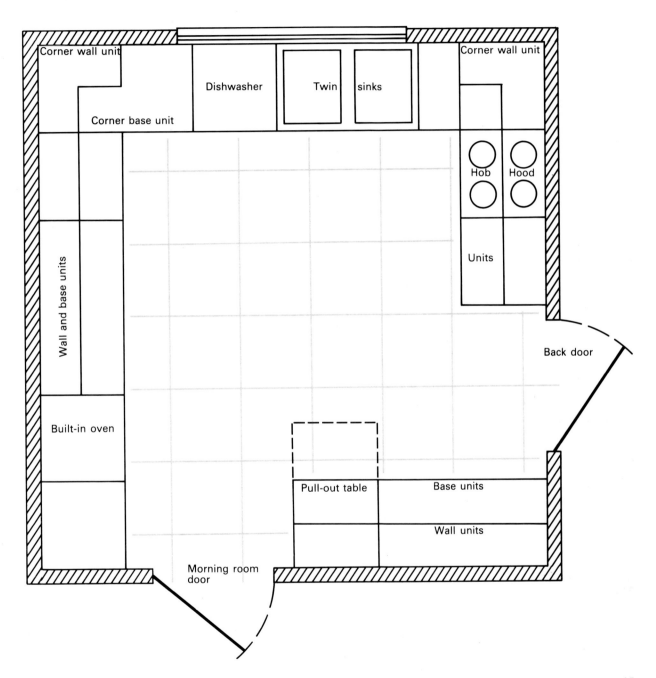

Corner wall unit

Corner wall unit

Dishwasher

Twin   sinks

Corner base unit

Hob   Hood

Wall and base units

Units

Built-in oven

Back door

Pull-out table

Base units

Wall units

Morning room door

⌂ *Another layout illustrating how versatile a simple square kitchen can be. (Ideal Home)*

◊ *A pull-out table is ideal for this busy family's breakfast and snacks. (Ideal Home)*

◊ *Mock Tudor beams in this living room/kitchen provide a natural break between living and working areas.*

a comfortable living room-cum-kitchen as a refuge in which to escape and relax (right). By incorporating these substantial outside-opening store cupboards and taking some 750 mm of the adjacent garage space, a comfortable kitchen and

living room could be created. All the internal walls were demolished and the rear wall of the garage moved forward. The resultant redesigned shape lent itself to all the demands of the family.

As the drawings show, the plan was quite radical and the family adventurously accepted all the recommendations.

The sink and the hob were placed in an unusual combination. Although the hob is almost at the end of the run of units, there is generous space around it as it is set forward to form a natural break between the working kitchen and the living area. This work surface ensures that there is no danger from projecting pan handles. The fridge/microwave housing unit is unconventionally sited next to the oven – again providing a divider between cooking and eating areas. Behind the oven, but opening out into the working kitchen, is the larder unit.

All the cooking and refrigeration equipment is built into brick housings. These reach short of the ceiling and striplights are fixed on the top to provide diffused light onto the ceiling. Beams and rough cast walls blend well with the mock Tudor beams on the house exterior.

◊ *Before the transformation, the ample floor space was mainly taken up with unused garden and fuel store, leaving only a small kitchen.*

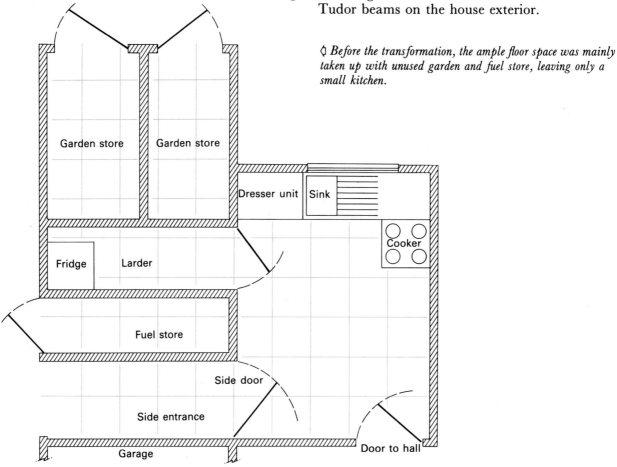

Garden store Garden store

Dresser unit | Sink

Cooker

Fridge Larder

Fuel store

Side door

Side entrance

Garage Door to hall

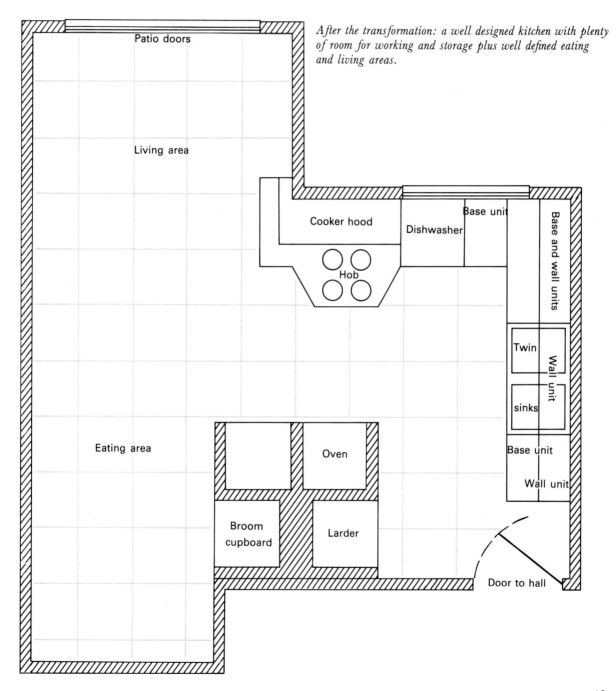

After the transformation: a well designed kitchen with plenty of room for working and storage plus well defined eating and living areas.

Patio doors

Living area

Cooker hood

Base unit

Dishwasher

Base and wall units

Hob

Twin

Wall unit

sinks

Base unit

Eating area

Oven

Wall unit

Broom cupboard

Larder

Door to hall

A kitchen for entertaining

There were no children in this household and the owner enjoys entertaining a constant stream of visitors.

Laundry equipment and the central-heating boiler were moved to a nearby utility room. The boiler left a chimney breast and recess which had been used for a flue and the question was whether to demolish it or leave it as a focal point. It was allowed to remain and the built-under oven and hob unit were inset here in an alcove of rustic tiles. The chimney breast surround was faced off with bricks and the whole cooker area was reminiscent of an old kitchen range.

Between the kitchen and the front of the house was a small breakfast room/study. Although the kitchen was an ample sized room, the wall between the two rooms was demolished and an archway formed in its place. The rear window of the kitchen overlooked the large garden and the owner chose to add a conservatory to the house with access from the kitchen. In place of the window in the back wall, large sliding glass doors were substituted between the kitchen and the new conservatory filled with tropical greenery. The resulting transformation, meant that only two walls remained on which to mount kitchen units.

The room therefore lent itself to an island unit about 1200 mm wide and 2400 mm long. This became the centre of activity serviced by the cupboards on the two walls, and storage under and above the island. This unit accommodated the one-and-a-half bowl sink, dishwasher, shelves and cupboards. The worktops and sinks for the island unit were made of a unique material, Corian, which can be designed to any size or shape. It copes with pastry-making, chopping and even plant-care with no sign of deterioration. One end of the worktop was designed to extend

⌂ *The rounded archway separates the working kitchen from the dining area.*

◊ *The island activity centre in white Corian is the heart of the kitchen. The hob is ingeniously set into the chimney breast.*

beyond the island unit to store two chairs underneath. Suspended above the island is an oval-shaped iron frame holding all the cooking pans and utensils on S-shaped hooks.

On the wall of the kitchen opposite the chimney breast is the large fridge/freezer and a butcher's block. The decor is enhanced with a mass of glass storage jars holding pastas, colourful dried beans and plants hanging from the ceiling. A shelf running at high level along this wall above the fridge holds more plants interspersed with discreet lighting to aid growth. The ceiling plasterboard was removed to expose the joists. These the owner painted herself and then finished them by rag-rolling.

These are a small selection of ways of utilising the space in what is essentially the same basic square-shaped room. You may not have a square-shaped room like this, but these examples illustrate that there are many possible permuta-tions for a simple-shaped room, depending on the needs of the householder. There is no need to be hide-bound by 'normal' kitchen layouts. Forget your pre-conceptions, analyse your own needs and design the kitchen to suit you.

Chapter 8

How to Do It

Our objective in this chapter is to ensure you have a basic understanding of what is involved in creating a new kitchen – whether you are doing it yourself or handing it over to a team of contractors. Having read this far, you should have an idea whether you are going to extend, knock down walls or make structural alterations of any kind. You should also have answered the questions on page 21 and defined your particular needs.

First, obtain some graph paper, pencil, rubber and a steel rule. Carefully measure your kitchen area and mark the dimensions to scale on the graph paper. Mark in the heights and positions of doors, windows and any items that cannot be moved, such as pipes or a central-heating boiler.

Divide the room into zones – working kitchen, utility and eating, as explained in Chapter 2. Remember the work sequence as set out in that chapter. On a separate sheet draw and then cut out scale outlines of your appliances, or even make models, and move them around the plan to see how it would work.

Units

Standard depth of worktop is 600 mm, to fit over

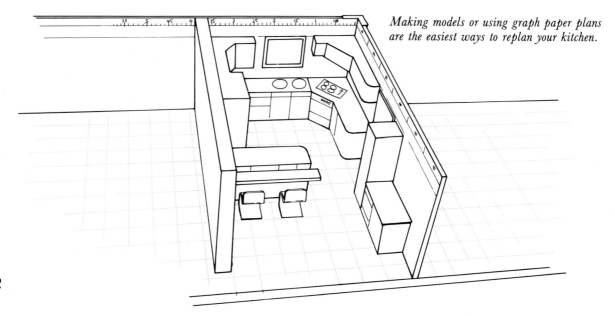

Making models or using graph paper plans are the easiest ways to replan your kitchen.

base units and appliances of the same or slightly shallower depth. But some equipment, like a dishwasher, may need a deeper worktop to accommodate the plumbing at the back.

Laminate worktops come in any depth up to 900 mm and are priced accordingly. A textured finish laminate worktop will withstand scratches and marks better than a smooth finish.

Post-formed, or curved, edges are easier to clean and less prone to damage than squared edges. But post-formed edges need very careful handling when mitreing corners and joints.

Make sure the core of the worktop is marine quality as this has a higher degree of water resistance. However, joints must be butted very tightly. If the sides of the worktops to be butted have an edging strip, this should be removed before butting up otherwise water and dirt could penetrate.

It is vital to seal the area between the sink and the worktop, also between the worktop and the wall or tiles, with a flexible sealant which will resist shrinkage.

Consult any kitchen unit catalogue and it will list sizes and heights of units, all based on a standard 600 mm module – 600 mm deep and 600 mm wide. Most cookers, fridges, dishwashers and washing machines will fit within this standard. Of course, units may be narrower or wider from side to side than this, but they are rarely a different depth from front to back.

Solid wood doors on kitchen units could prove troublesome if they are not made from properly seasoned wood. These doors, often constructed with a separately inserted centre panel, are prone to warp and split if exposed to damp. Conversely, a centrally heated atmosphere may make them shrink. However, if the wood has been kiln dried to a moisture content of 10 to 12 per cent, and fitted into a frame that allows movement in a normal kitchen atmosphere, it should be suitable for your kitchen. The higher priced units generally meet these standards. On a lower budget, a better choice would be laminate-faced units.

Planning the work

The length of time needed once the decision to transform the kitchen has been taken may be several months. Expect a month of total chaos during the ripping out of the old and installing the new. But remember that the more carefully you have planned the work, the easier and smoother the job will be.

At this point, it should be stressed that although you may wish to tackle all the work yourself, unless you are competent with technical understanding and highly skilled with ample time to spare, at least some jobs may be best left to the experts. By all means consult the professionals at this crucial stage to help you decide which tasks you can and cannot tackle. Obtain several estimates, and remember the words of John Ruskin who wrote:

'There is hardly anything in this world that some man cannot make a little worse and sell a little cheaper and those who consider price alone are this man's lawful prey!'

Before ordering the kitchen units, or hiring any experts, re-measure the kitchen. Check that your plan will fit the room. Check again and again and again!

When you are completely satisfied that all contingencies have been allowed for, order the units and appliances. Delivery may take eight or ten weeks. Prepare for the seige by cooking meals in advance to freeze and eat later during the upheaval. Empty cupboards of non-essentials. Discard old utensils, cracked dishes and any other 'heirlooms' you never use.

When work is due to start, establish a base camp in another room with your cooker and fridge temporarily connected and makeshift shelves or cupboards. Don't attempt to use the kitchen at this time. It can only result in disaster.

Structural work like knocking down walls, repositioning doors, windows and so on, should be done now.

Electrical work

If your electrical wiring is over 20 years old consult your Electricity Board or a qualified electrical engineer. All modern homes have a ring main circuit which is a single loop of cable to which any number of sockets can be connected. The cable used is 2.5^2 mm PVC sheathed twin and earth. Total loading is 7.2 kW, usually sufficient for all the appliances used in the home except for the kitchen and utility room. Here a washing machine, tumble dryer and dishwasher working at the same time would be too great a load for the circuit. Therefore there should be two separate ring circuits with as many outlets as possible and sockets for each appliance. It is as cheap to install double sockets as single ones and extra socket outlets are always useful.

Electric cookers must have their own circuit, using a minimum of 6^2 mm PVC twin and earth cable and 10^2 mm for the larger cooker, for example a free-standing double-oven model. The cooker control switch is fixed separately from the appliance and must be installed within two metres of it. One switch will operate a split-level electric cooker provided the oven and hob are within two metres of the switch. Many cooker control panels have an additional socket outlet in the panel but care should be taken when using it, as a lead to a nearby small appliance could so easily pass across the hob and cause an accident.

Sockets for percolator, toaster and other small appliances should be fixed flush to the wall about 200 mm above the worktop. Large equipment such as fridges and dishwashers need their own sockets. If the lighting cables are PVC it is wise to check that they have an integral earth wire.

If you have carried out the electrical work yourself be sure to consult a reliable and up-to-date source of information on specific electrical techniques and have the work inspected by your local Electricity Board.

Plumbing work

Water by-laws state that any fitting connected to a water supply must not misuse, waste or contaminate the mains supply. If a dishwasher and a washing machine are to be fitted, the hot and cold services may need extending, especially if the existing pipe diameters are too small to carry sufficient water to the draw-off points. It may be necessary to renew services right back to the hot water cylinder or cold water storage tank.

It is essential that access to the stop-cock inside the house is retained wherever it may be – on the wall or in a cupboard. Disguise it if you must, as in photographs (right).

The by-laws also require one tap – normally fitted in the kitchen – to supply drinking water only, i.e. connected to the mains.

If the mains water supply is still in lead or galvanised steel pipe, it could have become brittle or scaled up. Doubtful pipes should be checked and possibly replaced. If PVC water pipe is used, though, make sure your electrical supply remains properly earthed. If in doubt, consult an expert.

Position the pipework according to temperature; coldest at the bottom, hottest at the top so that the warming of mains water coming into the house is avoided.

Try to route piped services to other floors in

This neat spice rack swings out to reveal the stop cock.

the house through one channel so they may be conveniently boxed in, leaving an access panel in a suitable position.

When installing an automatic washing machine, check with the local water authority to see if the cold water supply must come from a water tank rather than the mains. Extra plumbing is required to connect the machine to the hot water supply and a waste pipe with a trap is required to convey the waste water. The bathroom is often a more logical place to site the washing machine. However, if you are plumbing the machine in the bathroom special electrical regulations must be followed. The machine must be permanently fixed and wired (without plug and socket) with a double pole switch. Controls on the machine must not be within reach of

someone in contact with a bath or shower, or wash basin, and all pipework, including that to the bath, must be earth bonded.

When installing a dishwasher, water pressure must lie between $100kN/m^2$ and $1000kN/m^2$, not a problem in most houses. Water pressure in some high rise flats may raise some problems, and where the cold water tank is on the same level as the dishwasher, it will not be possible to install a hot-fill model. Waste water is emptied by an electric pump and the outlet hose must rise at least above the level of the water in the dishwasher cabinet and to a maximum of 900 mm.

Check that those stylish Continental water taps at the kitchen sink do not contravene water by-laws, because some might. Further, you might find that the taps do not work satisfactorily in this country and the local water authority should be consulted.

Gas

Central-heating boilers, water heaters, cookers, ovens and hobs should always be installed by the local Gas Region service engineer or by a CORGI installer. A list of CORGI installers may be obtained from your Gas showroom.

Ensure you know where the gas main tap is located so it can be turned off easily and quickly in case of emergency.

Plastering

Although plastering looks simple, it takes a craftsman to make a good job of it so most people employ a professional for this job. The whole area must be carefully sounded for hollowness or lack of adhesion, before commencing. Any decaying or loose sections must be carefully cut out and made good. The surface must be clean, sound and dry before any attempt at plastering is made.

Flooring

A worn or sloping floor quickly induces fatigue in those walking on it. Sound preparation of the sub-floor ensures a hard-wearing floor in the long run. The sub-floor should be dry and clean, level and stable. Holes and cracks must be repaired. If you are laying a new concrete sub-floor, a permanent damp-proof membrane must be laid, as moisture will affect the floor months after installation. A wooden floor should be adequately ventilated to avoid dry rot. To prevent the impression of floor boards from showing through sheet vinyl, either plywood or hardboard should be fixed down to the sub-floor.

A vinyl floor should be laid after the kitchen units are fixed as joinery work could accidentally damage the flooring. To provide easy access for servicing, flooring should be laid under the free-

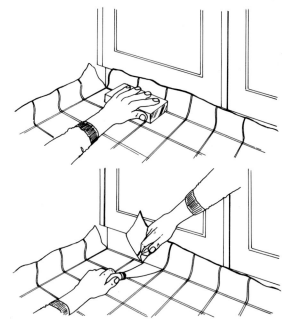

Lay vinyl flooring after the units have been fitted by pressing the sheet against the base of the unit then cutting with a sharp knife.

standing cooker, fridge, washing machine and dishwasher.

If hard quarry or ceramic tiles are to be used, fix them in advance so they are laid right under the fixed units, otherwise you may find the thickness of the tile may bring the moveable appliances up too high to fit under the work surfaces. Tiles can also be used on the plinths under the units so they match the floor.

Preparation for decorating

Woodwork can be prepared in advance. Walls, woodwork and any other surface can be given a coat of primer and sealed. When dry, the first undercoat can be applied. Top coats of paint should be applied when all the joinery work and unit fitting has been completed.

How to do it

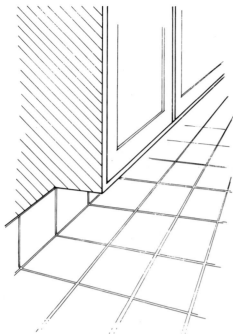

Tiles can be used on the plinths under the units.

Fitting the units

If it is necessary to adjust the height of the work-tops, the simplest way is to alter the plinths of the base units. Many units come with adjustable legs, concealed on completion by the plinths, which can be raised or lowered a few millimetres.

If you are taller than average, the legs can be raised on blocks to the required height. The plinths may cover the blocks, but you may need to conceal a wider gap and this can be successfully achieved by continuing the vinyl flooring up the face of the plinths.

Units should not be fixed into position until you have marked exactly which units go in which position in relation to the services (gas, water and electricity) already installed. Place them around the walls first to make certain that they fit – even at this stage a unit might be the wrong

To avoid unnecessary tile cutting, position wall units an exact number of tiles above the work surface.

size and may need to be changed or modified.

If you are tiling the walls, wall units should be placed exactly four, five or even six tiles above the worktop so that unnecessary tile cutting is avoided.

Worktops should be ordered slightly oversized so they can be cut down on site. If your walls are slightly uneven, tiling can cover a multitude of sins, merely by varying the thickness of the tile adhesive. Tiles can also be used to bridge the gap where the worktops of the base units do not fit tight to the wall.

Cut outs for sinks and hobs can be cut with a jigsaw into the worktops placed onto base units and connections made to their various supplies. Adjoining surfaces are held together by bolts through the core of the worktops, which adjust from underneath to make a tight join.

57

⌂ *Worktops can be cut out with a jigsaw to fit single or double sinks.*

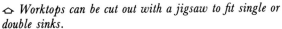

◊ *Plain white tiles can be enhanced by using coloured grouting to match the units.*

◊ *This quarry tiled floor has been extended upwards under the unit plinths to give an unusual and attractive effect.*

Finishing the job

The cooker can then be connected to gas and/ or electricity; the fridge placed in position and plugged in. Machines can be connected to water and electricity where applicable. Electrical work should be completed ensuring that screws fixing electrical sockets to the wall are long enough to go through tiles, if these have been used. On completion, the Electricity Board should be asked to inspect the installation to check it for electrical safety.

If the walls have been replastered, make sure the plaster is mature and thoroughly dry before fixing any tiles. Grouting should be applied about 24 hours after the tiles have been fixed. Use a brush to sponge and fill the gaps completely, wiping off the surplus grout immediately. When the grout has set, polish the tiles with a dry cloth. Although grout is usually white, it can be obtained in a colour to match either units or tiles. The effect in the pale green kitchen above has been enlivened by green grout on plain white tiles.

It would be impossible to cover every eventuality in this chapter, but hopefully it has pointed you in the right direction and indicated the key factors of concern. Do not be deceived into thinking that doing a kitchen yourself is simple. You must be prepared for a difficult task which may take longer and present problems which were not anticipated. If you do go ahead, however, you will have achieved a result that will give you and your family great satisfaction.

Chapter 9

Case Histories

Introduction

Complete kitchens should never come 'off the peg'. Every kitchen is different because every household is different – small or large families, a single person, a group of adults and children – almost any combination, in fact, with almost any lifestyle. Added to this, the family or household group will have different needs in, say, ten years' time, and different budgets available for the work to be done.

Of the hundreds of kitchens that Roma Jay has planned, we have taken eighteen examples to illustrate the variety of family sizes and needs, and the range of budgets available.

The size of the kitchen is not necessarily the crucial factor. A spacious kitchen can be just as inconvenient as a very small kitchen if the layout is bad and if it does not meet the needs of the people who use it. All the case histories described here are actual living, working kitchens, but you should not assume that any of them will perfectly match your unique requirements. The intention is to help you to analyse your own requirements and see the tremendous range of possibilities open to you.

No one should ever go into a kitchen showroom and say, 'I'll have one of those', pointing at a complete kitchen layout. Rather, you need to have a good understanding of what you need in relation to how you live, the size of the family unit, and the lifestyle.

Simple planning

These two examples were kitchens which required simple replanning and the minimum of structural alterations.

Planning around a central-heating boiler

The main problem that a Scottish couple and their adult son encountered in their kitchen was a gas central-heating boiler placed high on one of the outside-facing walls. Access for servicing had to be available on one side of the unit. Had the kitchen been planned before the central heating installation, a more suitable location could perhaps have been found for it, but that was not the case.

The family wished to eat in the kitchen, whilst the dining room was to be used for entertaining once or twice a month. Home baking was done weekly. The budget for the kitchen transformation was moderate. The other main criticism of their existing arrangements was lack of cupboard space.

The equipment and cupboards were deployed as follows. A narrow fridge/freezer was placed to the left of the back door with, next to it, the built-in oven, and the central-heating boiler with the work surface of the corner base unit underneath. This joins flush with the double-bowl sink unit underneath a wide window. To the right of the sink unit is the dishwasher with work surface over, which continues round into another corner base unit with wall cupboards above. Beside this is the electric hob with ducted extractor hood above it. The hob is linked to the remaining storage with a base unit which continues round into a peninsula with a higher level breakfast bar on the opposite side, giving room for family meals.

The boiler was considered 'a bit of an eyesore' and the owners wished to house it in a cupboard or camouflage it in some way. This was feasible because it was a room-sealed model. A flap-up door matching the new kitchen units was fitted to a batten framework to the right of the boiler providing easy servicing access and 'losing' the front of the boiler by merging it in with the false unit door.

Recipe testing

A cookery book author who needed a kitchen in which to test and photograph recipes, required

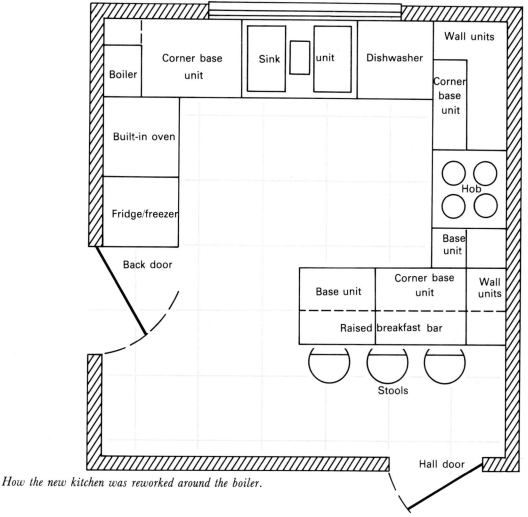

How the new kitchen was reworked around the boiler.

A kitchen does not have to be large to have ample work and storage space. The working side of this kitchen includes Corian sinks and worktops, and an extra pull-out worktop for extra space when recipe testing.

a rather special kitchen design. It had to be simple and uncluttered, yet have sufficient space in the cupboards to hold her collection of china and glass, spices and herbs collected from around the world.

The kitchen, in an Edwardian terraced house with grand proportions, was originally a study or dining room. The two ground floor rooms were divided by inter-communicating doors; the front room used for dining, and the back room containing the working kitchen.

As there was a chimney alcove already there, it made a good focal point for the room and the hob could have been set into it. However, this cookery book writer decided against this, as she wanted the room to be as clean and uncluttered as possible.

Access to the garden was through French doors at the end of the rear room, thus leaving only two walls free for kitchen units. She was adamant that she did not want an island unit because she felt it would get in her way. She was quite content with the two rows of units, provided there would be plenty of wall-hung storage space above the worktop.

As the ceilings were so tall, it was decided to fix wall cupboards fairly high, but with 'high-tech' open shelves between them and the work-tops. These were used for dishes completed for photography and for utensils in use, leaving the worktops free for work in hand.

One wall houses the dishwasher, two sinks, hob and built-in oven. An extra worktop pulls out of one of the base units between the hob and

The desk area at the end of the worktop is ideal for this author's kitchen. Drawers and cupboards provide ample storage space.

sink for the maximum amount of work space.

On the opposite wall is the fridge/freezer/chiller, base and wall units. Shelves were suspended underneath the wall units, and a desk area included for making quick notes on the recipes while testing.

Corian worktops and sinks help the clean, uncluttered lines of this kitchen and were chosen because the owner wanted something tough, hard wearing, practical and easy to care for.

The cork floor softens the room, is easy on the feet and has a touch of green which harmonises with the green shelves and handles of the otherwise white kitchen.

Shape solutions

Small, awkward-shaped kitchens can present special problems. These examples show how these virtually unworkable kitchens were transformed into labour saving dreams.

Five walls

A tiny kitchen in an old end-of-terrace house in a garden suburb presented a challenge with three windows and five walls, none of which was of equal length.

The new owner was a busy professional woman who lived with her teenage daughter. Breakfast and evening meals were to be eaten in the kitchen. Maximising on the microwave and the freezer, they entertained friends about once a month. The budget for this kitchen was moderate.

The previous occupants had fitted some units which had suffered from misuse. The double-drainer sink unit was against an inside wall

◊ ◊A two-way divider unit separates the working and eating areas in this unusual-shaped cottage style kitchen. (Ideal Home)

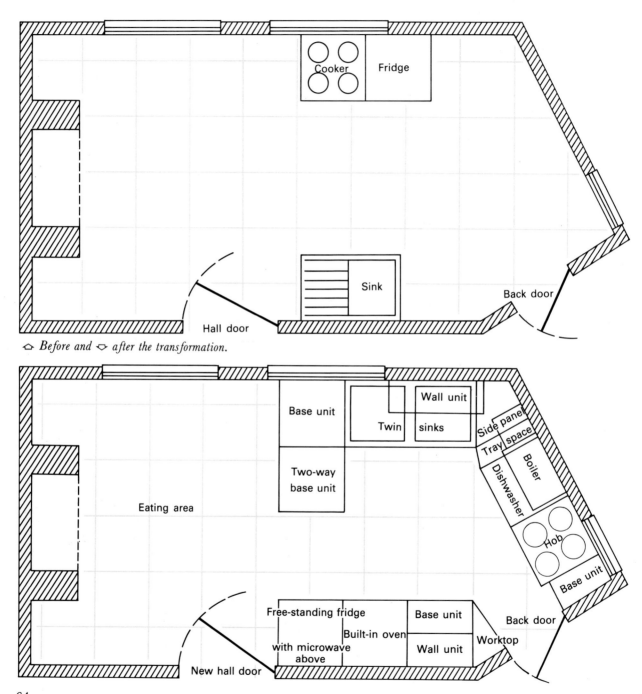

⬥ *Before and* ⬦ *after the transformation.*

which complicated the plumbing to the drains. A free-standing cooker stood in one corner near the door which led to the tiny utility room and toilet.

As there was no separate dining room in this compact, cottage-style house, the new kitchen had to provide an adequate eating area. A fridge/ freezer, built-in oven, base and wall unit are sited along the wall where the sink was originally placed. The owner's invaluable microwave oven, so useful for speedy suppers after work, was built in above the fridge so as not to take up scarce worktop space.

The new wall-hung central-heating boiler, which also provides whole-house hot water, is fixed on the angled wall in the kitchen. The gas hob sits beneath it on base units alongside the dishwasher. These are linked to the twin sinks under one of the windows whilst the peninsula under another window forms the division between dining area and kitchen. This peninsular base unit opens two ways for easy access from both sides.

Beyond the kitchen through louvred doors, the utility area holds dryer, washer and upright double-door freezer. Narrow shelves hold cleaning materials; and hooks were fitted to suspend brooms and floor mops etc.

Corridor kitchen

This kitchen was in a large Victorian house converted into flats. The rooms were gracious and the ceilings high, but the kitchen was a monstrosity only 1.7 metres wide and 2.4 metres long. There were many pipes running at crazy angles, some old and nasty tiling and dark, peeling paint. The victim of much make-do-and-mend, the kitchen was not much wider than a corridor. However well it could be decorated and designed, it was still an extremely small and narrow room.

The family consisted of two adults, a teenage son, an au pair and a huge red setter. The wife was American and she was used to a large fridge/ freezer, which in such a small kitchen would be difficult to accommodate. She also wanted a dishwasher, built-under oven and hob, separate grill, plus as many units as could be fitted in.

The family wished to increase the feeling of space, and so the kitchen was treated as one room with the long, narrow hall which led into it. The gloomy hall had six doors and a cupboard, and two levels of ceiling. The door between the two rooms was removed and replaced with a narrower archway. This gave more space in the kitchen for the 600 mm depth of the fridge/freezer alongside the archway. The opposite, long side of the kitchen only allowed a depth of 350 mm. The main working area of the room was, therefore, along the fridge/freezer wall. This consisted of a base unit, built-under oven, hob and dishwasher. Tall wall units were fitted above them.

One of the twin sinks fitted into the corner base unit while the other fitted over a standard 600 mm base unit modified to accept the waste pipes.

Wall units, 300 mm deep, were fitted onto plinths and used as base units along the narrower side of the room. 'High-tech' open shelves were fitted above the worktop thus giving extra storage space for foods, condiments and spices.

White units with green handles and shelves were chosen for maximum light and space. The floor and wall tiles are also white and the wallpaper in the hall is a soft green.

The austerity of the 'high-tech' look is relieved by a pretty white festoon blind, trimmed with green gingham. The transformed hall now has a small table which can be used for informal meals. The ceiling was levelled and lowered, creating a welcoming hall out of a previously grim entrance.

Extended ideas

More ambitious ideas and budgets to match are illustrated by these four kitchens where extensions were constructed and living rooms incorporated.

Family planning

Two adults, two teenagers and two young children made up this family who planned an extension to their home to contain a completely new kitchen. There was a separate utility room for the washing machine, but the existing floor-standing gas central-heating boiler had to stay where it was. They wanted to eat in the kitchen at a breakfast bar to seat up to eight people; they liked a rustic look, and were able to spend a reasonable amount to get the kitchen the way they wanted.

Three meals a day were eaten, plus home baking at least once a week, batch cooking for the freezer once a month; dinner party and other entertaining from time to time. This family had thought deeply about what their real needs were.

They specified a split-level oven and separate hob – both gas; they wanted to build in their refrigerator, dishwasher and microwave. They wanted ample sink space and a waste disposal unit, but felt that with a dishwasher there was no need for drainers.

The spacious extension measuring four metres by three metres allowed most of the family's requirements to be incorporated. The only item which had to be rethought was the location of the serving hatch into the adjacent dining room

▷◁ A feeling of spaciousness is created in this narrow hall and kitchen by removing the connecting door. Careful design allows for efficient working and maximum light, while the decor links the rooms and makes a welcoming hall from what was a dull corridor.

66

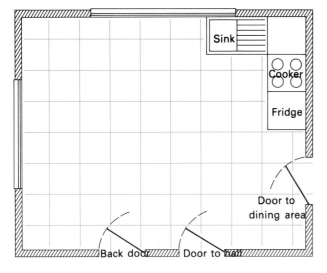

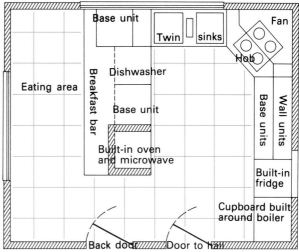

⌂ Before and ⇗ after, the new kitchen has plenty of room for meals, baking and entertaining.

⇗ A dream kitchen replaces a burnt-out shell.

where the formal entertaining took place.

The gas hob bisects the corner with a rustic style extractor hood and fan over it. Placing it across the corner provides more working space around and even behind the hob. The peninsular unit accommodates the dishwasher, base units and a breakfast bar. At one end of the peninsular unit is a brick housing for the oven. The work surface there is extra wide, and the dishwasher is fitted conveniently close to the eating area.

Fire nightmare into dream kitchen

Only ten years after it was built, the kitchen and utility room of this house was gutted by fire caused by faulty electrical wiring. After the shock had worn off, the owners welcomed the opportunity to install a safe electrical system and also to put in a well planned kitchen to suit their needs.

The original kitchen had been arranged around five walls with an archway into a large utility room. There was a large walk-in larder set well away from the working area. The oblong utility room was an ideal shape for an efficient kitchen. Outside the kitchen and backing onto the utility room was an open paved courtyard and a rarely used WC.

The new scheme involved some structural work, made almost easier by the fire. A half wall between the kitchen to the old utility room was removed making it one with the kitchen. The courtyard was roofed over and a wall built which then became the new utility room.

Ingenious use was made of the old walk-in larder which conveniently backed onto a outside-facing wall. A partition was built to bisect the space, the back part was used to house the meters with an access hatch which opened outside the house for meter reading. The front was still deep enough to house the fridge and built-in oven.

Alongside the oven is the dishwashing zone consisting of base and wall units, dishwasher and single sink.

To provide a visual link between the kitchen and dining area, the hob was set into an extra deep base unit and a rustic hood covering the extractor unit fitted over it. Recessed into the wall behind the hob is a small, antique lead fire surround. In the old kitchen area, with its five walls, a spacious and bright dining area has been created.

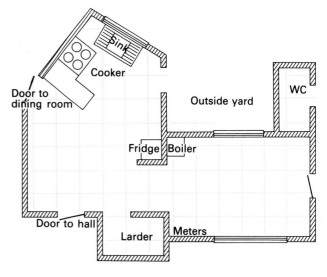

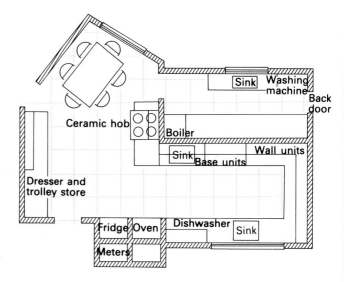

↔ *Structural alterations, as in this fire-damaged kitchen, can give extra freedom for kitchen redesign and allow space which was wasted before to be incorporated into the kitchen area.*

68

Storage space re-used

A 1961 built chalet bungalow which originally suited its young family, became less convenient as the two children grew into young adults needing more room to entertain their own friends.

Behind the large garage was an integral store room and fuel store. The garage was linked to the house beside the entrance hall and another door from the garage led to a little courtyard at the back of the house.

An architect-designed extension covered in this courtyard and incorporated the outside store room into habitable space. The new kitchen was moved into the newly created room and an archway from the hall led into the original courtyard.

This had a new glass domed roof which gave masses of light and was used as a breakfast room and filled with plants as well as garden furniture.

The new working kitchen was planned into a U-shape with beige laminate and wood units fitted around the walls. To add a focal point, the ceramic hob was fitted onto a base unit brought forward from the line of units. A hood was built over it to conceal the extractor fan. The appliances fitted into the room were a built-in double oven, dishwasher, double bowl sink and drainer, built-in fridge.

The wall units did not reach the ceiling, so striplights were fitted above them to illuminate the ceiling with a soft, diffused light. Decorative objects and plants standing on top of the units benefit from the light behind.

▷ This tiny kitchen did not suit the occupants, so they decided to make structural alterations and incorporate the courtyard and store rooms to create a larger working kitchen, open living and dining area and separate utility room.

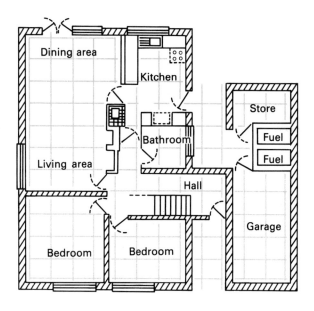

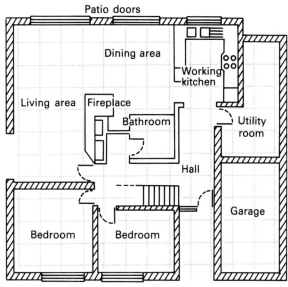

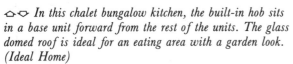

⬦⬦ In this chalet bungalow kitchen, the built-in hob sits in a base unit forward from the rest of the units. The glass domed roof is ideal for an eating area with a garden look. (Ideal Home)

▽◁ △ Three views of this Kosher kitchen show how the double-sided divider neatly separates the working and eating areas of the kitchen.

The built-in oven is surrounded by storage space, and the two dishwashers are built in to match the units. The sinks and worksurfaces are Corian.

71

Kosher cuisine

The family in this household comprised parents, three children and an au pair. An elderly parent came to stay at regular intervals. Cooking and entertaining are an important part of this family's life and their existing morning room and kitchen just couldn't cope with the demands made on it. The owners decided to extend across the whole width of the morning room and kitchen at the back of the house.

They required a living room, an informal dining room and a Kosher kitchen. According to Jewish dietary laws, milk and dishes deriving from dairy foods may not be mixed or eaten with meat. Those observing Jewish dietary laws keep separate utensils for cooking milk/dairy food meals and meat meals. Separate cupboards and drawers store utensils, cutlery, crockery and the foods themselves. For those who do not have the space or the money to do this, divisions can be made in units and drawers, but errors can be made. The fridge can have separate milk and meat shelves and this works well.

With dishwashers there is controversy. Some religious authorities maintain that the temperature at which the dishes are washed ensures that particles of the different foods do not contaminate crockery and cutlery. Others insist that a dishwasher can only be used for one category either milk or meat. This kitchen in fact holds two dishwashers.

The location of the kitchen within the area caused much family discussion, as well as many alternative plans. Eventually, with many misgivings, it was agreed to position it along the right hand side of the extension, making it a long, narrow room. Lack of light was the main stumbling block, but by installing a window overlooking the garden as well as one onto the side entrance, sufficient light shines through.

The side entrance door was moved to give easy access to the washing machine and dryer installed in the garage. The wall between the side and hall doors holds a ventilated larder, a wide fridge/freezer and a full length china cupboard.

The dining area is separated from the kitchen by a peninsula of two-way opening glass units suspended above the base units and a deep worktop.

At the side of the door is a dishwasher, double sinks, the second dishwasher, base units and hob, leading into the corner with more base units running under the window, facing the garden. Wall units are placed at safe heights above the hob and above the base units.

The worktops and sinks are in solid non-porous Corian which is particularly useful in this type of kitchen. It can be bonded to obtain an impermeable seamless surface. No cracks or crevices can harbour bacteria. The colour scheme of pale green and white gives a feeling of light and does not dominate the narrow room.

Space survey

Probably one of the greatest needs when improving kitchens is to create more space by repositioning walls, doors, windows and demolishing cupboards. The objective is to achieve more usable space without going to the expense of building an extension. These examples illustrate ways of achieving this end.

Window into doors

When this young couple wrote to *Ideal Home* magazine for advice on their kitchen, their first child was expected. The house, built in the 1920s, had a very large kitchen with windows overlooking the garden; a large walk-in larder and a big utility room. In fact the house was featured in the magazine during the 1930s.

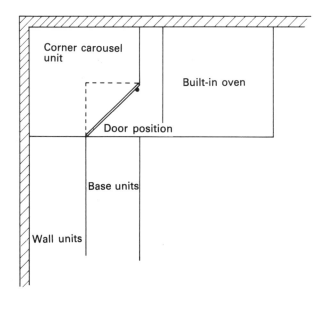

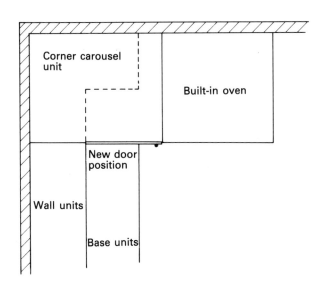

A plan section illustrating a corner unit modification.

An interior designer herself, the owner only needed a kitchen planning expert to provide the key to spark off her own creative ideas to revamp the kitchen. In this case, the key was to convert an existing window overlooking the garden into French doors, in order to give easy and safe access into the garden for the future family.

As soon as this idea clicked, the planning was simple. They chose French Mobalpa units which match the wood panelling of the rest of the house. Rough cast white walls contrasted well with the mid oak. (Photographs overleaf.)

A large alcove which formerly held the fridge and cooker was converted into a cooking range with the gas hob set into Corian work surface. The fridge was built under the work surface and deep drawers hold pans and cooking utensils. The large collection of herbs and spices sit on the beam above the breast.

This true family room has space enough for the baby's playpen, as well as a corner containing cookbooks, TV, shelves, in fact a mini-desk space.

Even in the best planned kitchens unexpected problems occur, and it is the skilful fitter who will turn such disadvantages around. A small gap between the corner wall carousel unit and the adjacent oven housing unit would normally be filled by an infill panel. But the ingenuity shown by this fitter created a convenient tray storage at high level.

Larderectomy

A designer's nightmare could best describe this odd shaped kitchen in a block of mansion flats. Six walls, two doors, and a triangular shaped walk-in larder, plus pipes and pipe ducts wasting valuable wall space.

The owner was a business woman living alone, but with frequent visitors and overnight guests. Informal meals were eaten in the kitchen with as

73

⌂ *The young couple's kitchen before the transformation was unattractive and wasted valuable floor space.*

◊ *Removing the old window and making a new doorway gives easy access to the garden.*

▽ *The working area of the kitchen utilises the alcove for a cooking range with deep drawers for pans and utensils.*

◊ *This awkward-shaped kitchen was transformed by removing a rarely-used larder. Even so, the skilful fitter had to cope with some problems, such as the back wall running several degrees out of true.*

many as six people needing chairs. The washing machine had to be plumbed into the room, and a large fridge/freezer as well as a wide free-standing cooker had to be incorporated.

When the cupboards were removed and the curiously shaped walk-in larder removed, the room measured 3.6 metres by 3 metres wide. But the back wall ran several degrees out of true which made fitting extremely difficult.

To add to the fitter's difficulties were a gas meter high up on the wall adjacent to the back door; an electricity meter on the only wall that could take several wall units together; another pipe duct preventing units being fitted into the corner; and a set of pipes housed in an ugly casing near the back door.

The free-standing cooker was placed near the rarely-used back door which led to a fire escape. The Leisure single-drainer sink and waste bowl on a 1000 mm base unit was fixed between the cooker and washing machine on the angled wall under the window. Next to the washing machine base units were fitted with worktops above them. Wall units hang on this wall which have striplights fixed neatly into the underneath to illuminate the surface below. To give access to the meters and yet still provide sufficient cupboard space, the skilful fitter made a framework on which to mount the wall units.

On this same wall runs a cold water lead pipe

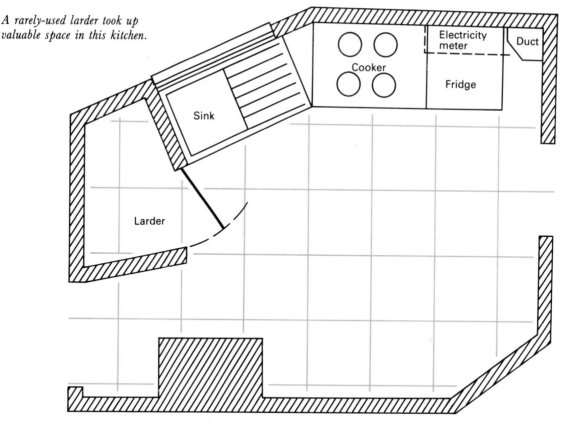

A rarely-used larder took up valuable space in this kitchen.

and stop cock. To disguise the pipe and still give access to the stop cock, the framework was extended down as far as the base units. A ceramic tiled panel covers the framework, and a spice shelf was ingeniously fitted into the panel which hinges out when necessary to reveal the stop cock. (Photographs page 55.)

The large fridge/freezer was placed opposite next to the hall doorway. Behind the fridge, on an angled wall, space was found to hang lightweight aluminium steps.

The large pipes carrying the block's central-heating system run through a large square duct in the kitchen. The recess on one side provides space for the dining table and chairs, whilst the wall on the other side holds a plastic grid on which household items can be hung.

Everything including the kitchen sink

A mother and her twenty-five-year-old son wished to improve the square unfitted kitchen in their home counties house. Built into the kitchen was a walk-in larder, and an outside store adjoined it. A free-standing gas cooker, washing machine, dryer, fridge/freezer and sink top were to be kept. They wanted another window and the room needed heating.

Breakfast and the evening meal were to be eaten in the room. Fitting and structural work was to be done by the handy son, so the small

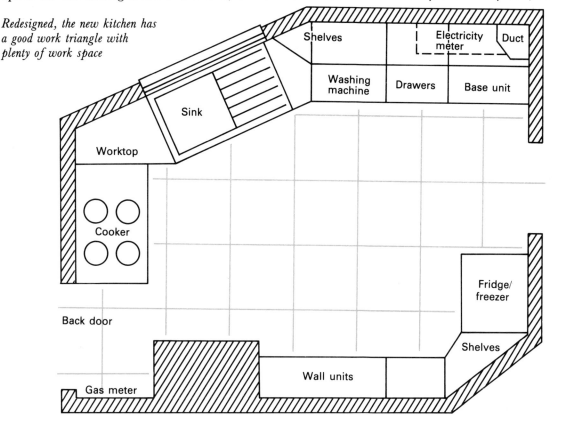

Redesigned, the new kitchen has a good work triangle with plenty of work space

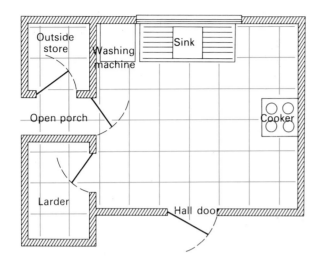

budget could be used for new units only.

The existing kitchen measured 3.6 metres by 3.4 metres. The structural work recommended was to remove the wall dividing the larder from the main kitchen; the outside door to the store was bricked up and the wall dividing it from the kitchen was demolished. The dryer and washing machine were placed side by side and a 60 cm deep worktop was fitted above both machines up to the cooker, in its new position between the washing machine and sink. As the existing sink top was only 50 cm deep, it would not line up with the new worktops and units, and it would harbour dirt and have sharp corners, so it was decided to invest in a new sink unit to match the rest of the units.

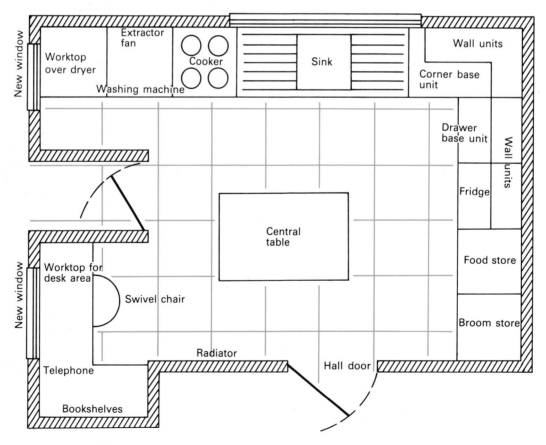

Along the wall which had previously housed a cooker, a more efficient workflow was established, consisting of base and wall units, fridge/freezer, food storage and broom cupboards.

The old larder area was turned into a home office with a worktop holding the telephone, shelves for cook books etc. A central-heating radiator fits snugly in the office.

New windows were fitted either side of the porch to increase the light. A dining table is placed centrally in the new kitchen.

Kitchen sculptures

Two large walk-in store cupboards dominated one end of this kitchen. The wife of the family is a sculptor and spends very little time cooking. But after many years of making-do she felt a complete change was necessary.

The family consisted of parents and two grown up children and a cat. Their dining room was used as a study, so they wanted to eat and entertain in the kitchen. With good natural light from the window overlooking a garden full of sculptures, the potential was great.

At the opposite end of the kitchen to the walk-in store cupboards, another two cupboards housed the washing machine and central-heating boiler. It was agreed not to remove these cupboards for the time being, as at a later date, when the boiler would be ready for replacement, a new boiler could be wall hung and the free space converted to a downstairs lavatory, blocking up the door directly from the kitchen/

◊ There was plenty of scope to improve this square unfitted kitchen. ◊ The larder was turned into a home office, still having ample space for the kitchen itself.

◊ ◊ The owner's sculptures enhance this compact kitchen and dining area.

diner and entering via the utility room.

To maximise the potential a fair amount of structural work was necessary. At the working end of the room, the two walk-in cupboards were demolished. The garden door was blocked up and replaced by a window. The existing window was converted into double French doors, allowing light from the garden to flood inside and to view the garden exhibition from inside.

This gave ample area for cooking and eating. However, as cooking was not the favourite pastime of the family, it was decided to make the kitchen as compact as possible. Beside the hall door is a Bosch fridge/freezer/chiller. Next to this is a larder and built-in gas oven with wall units reaching to the ceiling. The dishwasher is positioned under a tiled work surface. The gas hob and indoor barbecue grill are linked to the

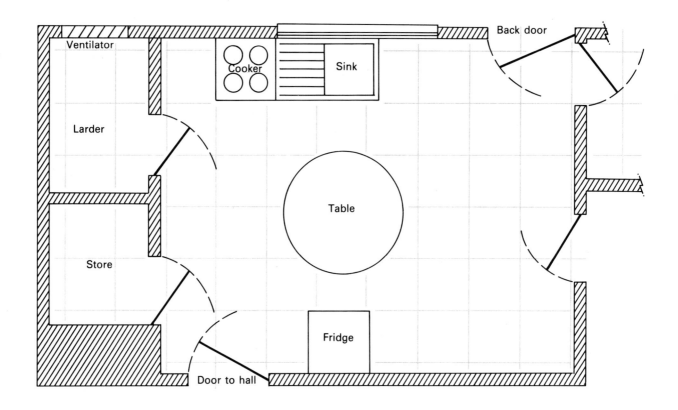

↶ Originally an inefficient layout, this sculptor's new kitchen ↻ is perfect for her family's needs.

peninsula holding the sink unit.

The U-shape was formed by a peninsular unit dividing the working and dining areas. The two-and-a-half-bowl sink fits into the worktop and a high bar was fitted above to provide extra work surface, as well as masking any clutter.

The dining area was sufficiently large for the table to be permanently in position for meals. Sculptures and paintings by the artist herself add individuality to the Bosch rustic wood units. The ceramic floor tiles ideally complement the hexagonal worktop and wall tiles and complete the country mood.

Lighting, so important to this artist, is a combination of pendant fittings, recessed spotlights over the working area and, most valuable, concealed striplights under the wall cupboards directly illuminating the cooking area.

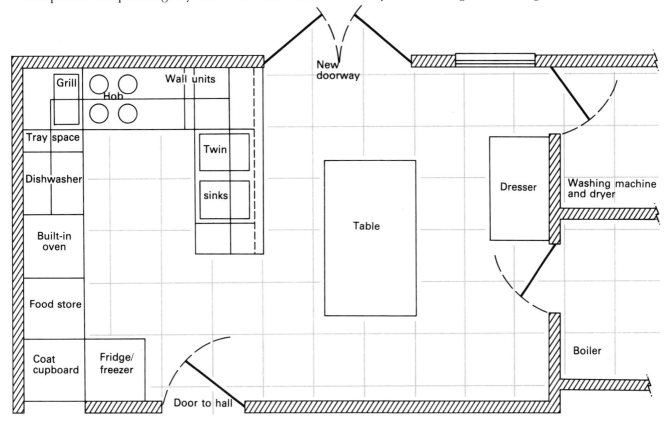

Do it yourself
The removal of a part wall and doorway between the kitchen and dining room gave this West Country family of two adults and three children

a generous new living space. Previously, the kitchen had been small with little natural light. Joining the two rooms added light from the south-west facing dining area window.

The owner is a do it yourself addict and enjoyed demolishing, with the help of his children, the built-in cupboards. He then built a new wall leading to the lounge which incorporated an archway from the kitchen/dining area.

The laundry equipment had to remain in the kitchen and the new layout incorporated all the plumbing along one wall.

The dryer is stacked above the washing machine and a base unit links them to the twin-bowl sink centred under the north-east facing window. To the left of the sink is the dishwasher and corner base unit, both of which have wall units above. The corner unit stores clean crockery taken from the dishwasher.

At right angles, the gas hob is fitted into the worktop which links up with the peninsular unit, backed by a raised bar in the dining area – ideal for breakfasts. On the opposite side of the kitchen, the fridge/freezer and built-in electric oven stand together.

The budget for this major re-jig was average, with the owner handling most of the structural and installation work himself.

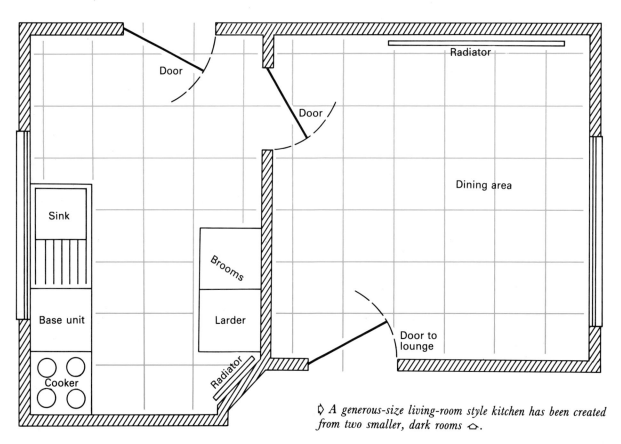

♀ *A generous-size living-room style kitchen has been created from two smaller, dark rooms* ◁.

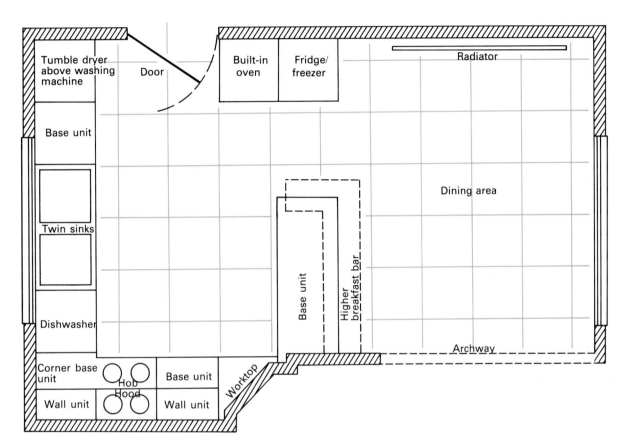

Tumble dryer above washing machine

Door

Built-in oven

Fridge/ freezer

Radiator

Base unit

Twin sinks

Dishwasher

Base unit

Dining area

Higher breakfast bar

Corner base unit

Hob

Hood

Base unit

Wall unit

Wall unit

Worktop

Archway

Space efficient

When this family of four moved into their new house in a fashionable part of London, they had no idea of how difficult it would be to fit the kitchen.

The room had a window, a deep recess and five doors which left no walls for fixing base and wall units. One of the doors led to a pantry, broom store, box room and WC. It was decided

Case histories

that the only way they could have an efficient kitchen and informal dining area was to demolish this cluster of small rooms, revealing a long narrow area – ideal for an efficient workflow. The family consisted of parents, two children, an au pair and a dog. The cellar housed their laundry equipment and boiler.

Space is put to far better use when the run of units is unbroken by doors and windows. Efficiency and a good workflow are easier to achieve: this new kitchen is a perfect example of a U-shaped arrangement (photographs overleaf).

The large recess in the original kitchen was deep enough to accommodate the fridge/freezer. This was linked to the main U-shape by quarter round open shelves. These adjoin the built-in oven, dishwasher, base and wall units, plus a sink forming a dishwashing zone. On the opposite wall, under the window, are base units linking to the barbecue grill and electric hob,

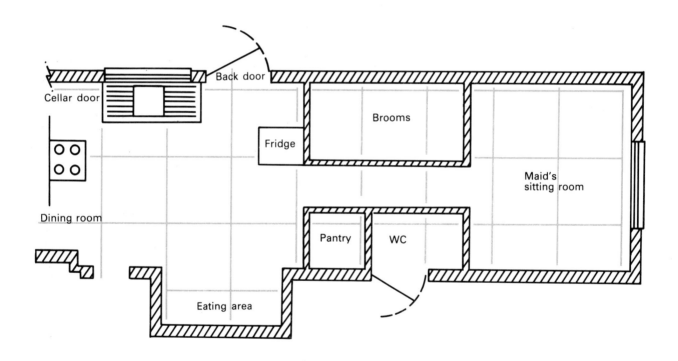

Five doors, plus an unused pantry and WC made this a nightmare kitchen for a family of four.

84

plus a preparation sink, base and wall units, a second built-in oven and microwave. The food preparation area is close to the food store.

The former kitchen becomes the new eating area with table and chairs sufficient to seat six people.

Limitations prove an advantage

This old house in the Kent countryside has always had a solid fuel range for cooking, hot water and heating. When planning to modernise the kitchen, the new owners replaced the old with an up-to-date solid fuel unit, which also provided central heating, hot water and cooking facilities.

The couple, in their thirties with two toddlers, wished to use the room for family meals, but felt that the original kitchen was untidy and unplanned. Budget for the transformation was fairly low.

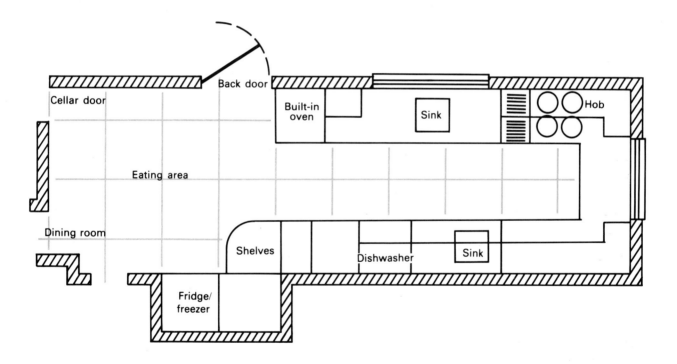

Completely reversing the old layout, the long U-shape is ideal for a space-efficient working kitchen, with a larger eating area for the family.

⌂ *A cluster of small rooms was re-planned into this efficient and fresh-looking kitchen. (Ideal Home)*

⇂ *A view of the garden and open shelves of plants give a garden atmosphere. (Ideal Home)*

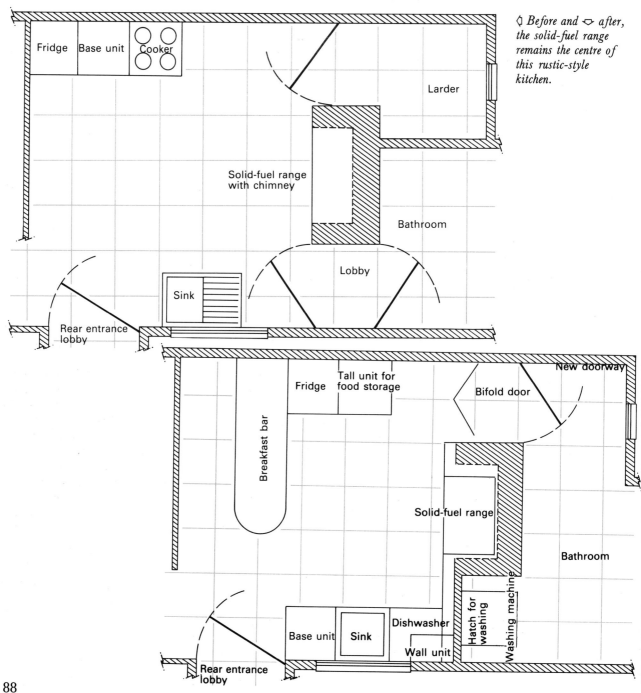

◊ *Before and* ◡ *after, the solid-fuel range remains the centre of this rustic-style kitchen.*

Fridge | Base unit | Cooker

Larder

Solid-fuel range with chimney

Bathroom

Lobby

Rear entrance lobby

Sink

Breakfast bar

Fridge | Tall unit for food storage

New doorway

Bifold door

Solid-fuel range

Bathroom

Base unit | Sink | Dishwasher | Wall unit | Hatch for washing | Washing machine

Rear entrance lobby

They wanted to keep the character of the country setting by restoring the old ceiling timbers and rough stone walls to achieve a comfortable rustic effect in the new kitchen.

Their existing dishwasher, washing machine and fridge/freezer were to be retained.

Adjoining the cooker alcove and directly behind the kitchen is a bathroom. At one side of the alcove was a little used walk-in larder, whilst the other side contained the door between kitchen and bathroom. To attain a better working area, it was decided to block up the door to the bathroom, but open a new doorway in the larder, which had been little used as a store cupboard. Two doors must always separate a kitchen from a WC, thus the larder became a lobby into the bathroom. By repositioning the bathroom door, wall space was created against which the washing machine could be plumbed inside the bathroom. A hatch in the wall between the two rooms meant that dirty linen could be pushed through to a waiting basket in the bathroom.

Solid floors prevented moving the sink from its original position. The sink could now be linked to the cooker by a continuous worktop with the dishwasher between the two. A wall unit to hold clean crockery was fixed over the dishwasher.

On the opposite side of the room a tall food store and fridge/freezer linked up to a peninsular unit with two-way cupboards and a breakfast bar. Extra wall units were placed above the fridge/freezer.

The safety factor in this kitchen where young children could easily become a hazard, had therefore been avoided. The traffic area to and from the bathroom had previously been within the cooking zone between the sink and hob. This dangerous route was diverted away from the cooking and preparation areas.

Bending the rules

Three growing daughters, a dog and an adult with a back problem were some of the factors governing the modernisation of this kitchen in a 50-year-old detached house. The room incorporated a number of walk-in cupboards and little else but a free-standing cooker, sink and fridge.

The head cook was keen but suffered from a bad back. She needed higher than normal work surfaces, a built-in oven and even a built-in dishwasher to avoid painful bending. The units were raised by fixing blocks underneath the plinths. Once all the walk-in cupboards were removed it cleared the decks for a completely fresh approach.

The ideal 'cooking circle' of 'storage – preparation – cooking – serving – dishwashing' could easily be applied and still allow ample space for a dining area for this family of five. Food storage close to the cooking area includes a fridge/freezer, narrow pull-out larder and two deep cupboards above the built-in oven and fridge/freezer.

Preparation and cooking of food takes place along a half wall between the kitchen and eating area: the four-burner gas hob and a single-bowl sink – saucepans and other utensils are stored in drawers under the hob. The half wall shields the cooking clutter from the dining area.

Casseroles and glass oven ware is stored under the built-in oven in deep drawers. Cake making equipment is kept alongside and the mixer sits on a lift-up shelf which swings down into the base unit when not in use. A two-plate ceramic hob is set into the worktop in this area.

The dishwashing zone runs along the window wall where twin round bowls, one containing a waste disposal unit, are set into worktops over base units. The dishwasher is housed in a unit which holds crockery.

Lighting was carefully planned – striplights were fitted into a recess under the wall units.

△ A rustic mood was chosen for this open plan dining area and kitchen, with careful lighting to set the right atmosphere. The beams hide unsightly pipes which could not be moved.

⌂ *The dishwashing zone runs under the window and houses a dishwasher and crockery storage space in the units. Clever use is made of a slim space as a tray store.*

The base shelf of the wall units was raised inside which then hid not only the striplights, but also the socket outlets. Trailing flexes are unknown and the ceramic tiles are not marred by banks of socket outlets.

The beams on the ceiling are not merely decorative. They box in some of the unsightly pipes which could not be removed. Warm cork floor tiles contribute to the feel of comfort in this spacious family kitchen.

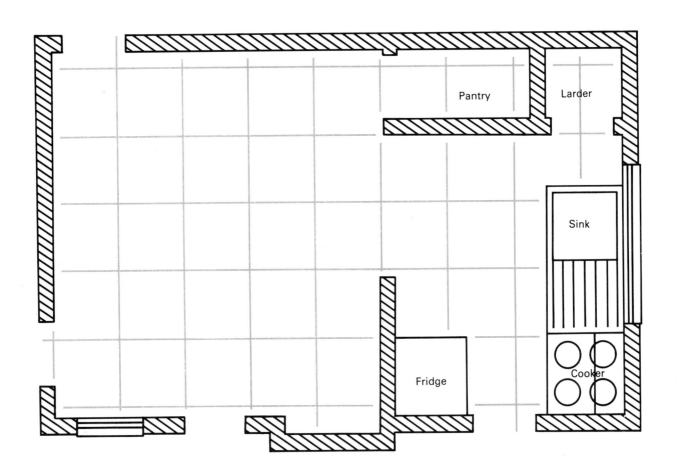

More efficient work and storage space was needed for this family of five, which the new layout ⟲ clearly provides.

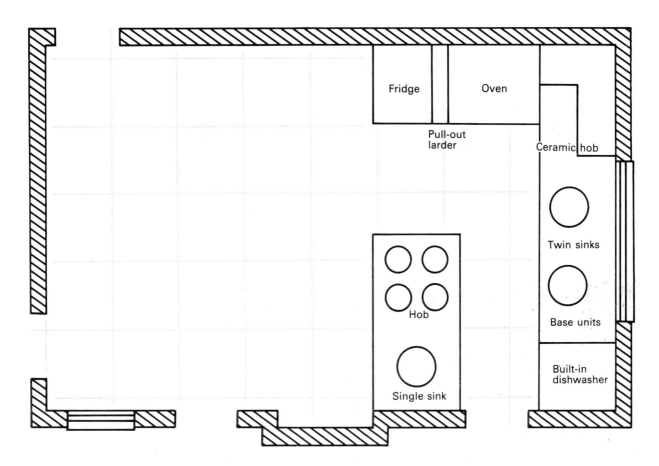

Restoration

This Hertfordshire residence, built in the 1920s, is a relic of a gracious era. It comprised two large reception rooms, large airy hall, butler's pantry, morning room, huge larder, kitchen and laundry room.

The family who moved into this house were parents and two pre-teenage children. Cooking and entertaining, as well as growing her own fruit and vegetables for freezing or preserving are this housewife's relaxation. She is also a keen junk shop addict – spotting objects that anyone else would reject. She then lovingly restores them not merely to their former glory, but improves on the original.

While she could see the potential of the house, she could not visualise the kitchen area with its maze of cupboards and rooms. As a designer it

93

is necessary to find out how the kitchen would be used and what the family's requirements are before producing a plan. During our discussions it became clear that cooking was a major part of the activities. The wife cooked not because it was expected of her, but because she truly enjoyed it. She seemed cut out for an Aga cooker, and once it was explained to her just what an Aga was about, she couldn't wait to try it. The gas-fired Aga is on continuously, heats the water in the kitchen and cloakroom and warms the kitchen. Once this was agreed, the plan for the kitchen seemed to fall into place.

The kitchen was to be the central focus of the home with eating and relaxing space for the entire family. A separate utility room was essential for all the clutter that families collect. Once planned, it was then possible to demolish walls, block up or open doors and reposition walls to create the space needed for each activity. The utility room was spacious enough to house the gas central-heating boiler, a huge chest freezer, washing machine, dryer, indoor propagating material, sink unit and various storage cupboards.

In the kitchen the Aga fits against the outside facing wall between two windows. To give it more character, a brick chimney was built to make it look like a cooking range. An extractor fan placed in the wall above, concealed by a rustic hood. The mantelpiece of a disused fireplace in the house has been used here to store spices, herbs and other cooking aids. Fixed under it is a dowel rod from which kitchen tools are suspended. Base and wall units are fitted on both sides of the range, with the table centrally positioned.

To match the farmhouse style, old beams were acquired and fixed to the ceiling. The walls and ceiling are painted with white rough cast paint. The floor is quarry tiled. The table and chairs were found in a junk shop and have been lovingly restored by the enthusiastic homemaker.

The finishing touch is that the wall tiles are unspoilt by sockets and plugs. Like the previous kitchen, the sockets are installed in a recess under the wall units.

◊ *Sockets and striplights under the base of the wall units avoids spoiling wall tiles.*

◊ *The Aga takes pride of place in this farmhouse-style kitchen where cooking is a major part of the family's activities.*

Passing through

This young couple bought a first floor flat in North London, and only planned to stay for two years before buying a house. As their budget was small they wanted to retain all their existing equipment. Cooking was one meal a day and friends were entertained for dinner about once a month. Batch cooking for the freezer was done fortnightly. Their main complaint was lack of work surfaces available and poor use of the adjoining room which contained only the washing machine.

As the budget was limited, the owners wished to keep their cooker, fridge and washing machine, as well as new pine units. The bulk of the spend was towards structural work to make the space more useable.

The partition wall between the utility room

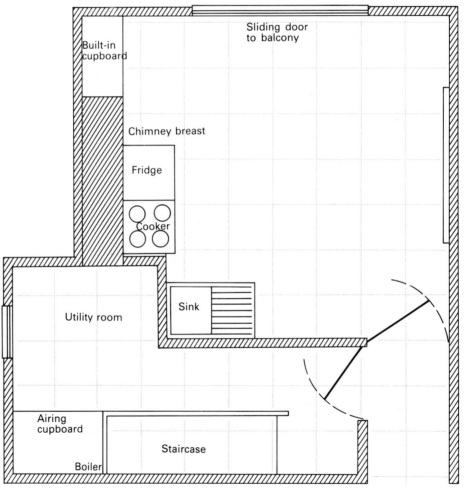

Plenty of space, but badly laid out, was the complaint here.

and kitchen was removed. This gave room for the front-loading washing machine to be relocated alongside the sink unit. A work surface was installed over it to meet the sink. To complete this run, a tray space was built on the other side of the sink unit, aligning it with the cooker placed behind the draining board. The under worktop freezer, existing base unit and extra worktop were all linked together to form a peninsula dividing the dining area from the kitchen. The freezer opens into the dining area.

Along the wall of the former utility room, backing onto the staircase, a narrow work surface only 46 cm deep is fitted alongside the existing refrigerator increasing the total work surface area considerably. A practical working kitchen, eating area and utility area has been created within a limited budget.

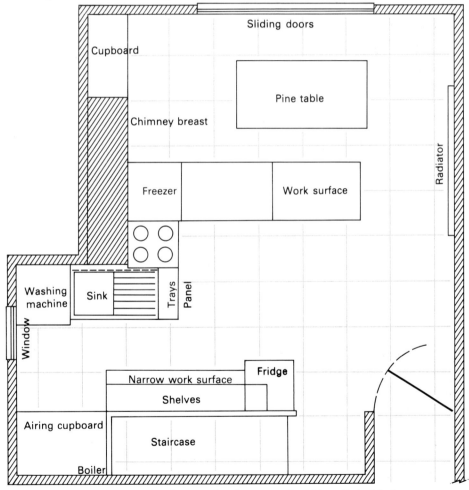

A practical working kitchen, eating area and utility area has been created within a limited budget.

Chapter 10

What's Right for You ~
Equipment Design

For the purposes of this book we conducted a qualitative survey amongst two hundred people, many of whom had installed new kitchens. The objective was to establish views about the design of equipment, and its suitability for use in the home. Our conclusions on the results of the survey have been incorporated into the following two chapters.

This chapter summarises our main recommendations on worktops, sinks and taps, waste disposal units, kitchen units, ovens and hobs, fridges and freezers, dishwashers and washing machines. We also highlight some new, untested products which may meet specific user needs.

Worktops

There are no hard and fast rules for worktop heights, wall units and tall storage cupboards – simply because people come in different sizes – so don't assume that you must have standard height work surfaces if that is not what you need. There are minimum storage facilities set down for local authority housing. These include dimensions of the units, but they don't relate to the height of the users. Thus the unit manufacturers decided for themselves what is the most convenient height. Co-operation does exist between the

unit manufacturers and the makers of domestic appliances which fit below or line up.

For many years the British worktop height has been 900 mm. Continental manufacturers vary their worktop heights from 820 mm up to 880 mm. However the height recommended for the user is 50 mm below the bent elbow whilst the user is standing.

◊ *A lower-level cooking range in a country style kitchen.*

◊ *The space between the worktop and the wall unit must pay for its keep.*

Tasks like stirring a saucepan are more comfortable 200 mm lower than the bent elbow; rolling pastry, which requires downward pressure should be 250 mm lower than bent elbows. Tasks like pouring soup into a liquidiser also need a lower level worktop. The practicalities of installing different levels of worktop can prove more trouble than it's worth, but some manufacturers are attempting it.

In many kitchens the wall units are fitted about 450 mm above the worktop to line up with the tops of tall housing units. But you can use the wall space between the base unit worktop and the wall unit more effectively, and waste less space above the units, by fixing wall units 600 mm above the worktop. This still allows easy access to the bottom and middle shelves, and leaves the wall below free to fix foil and cling film dispensers, kitchen paper, scales and even narrow shelves. This can be useful, especially in a small kitchen.

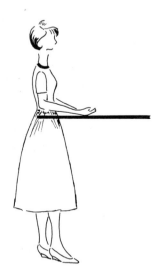

The recommended worktop height is 50 mm below the bent elbow while the user is standing.

Natural materials such as granite, slate, marble and wood have been satisfactorily used for worktops. Laminates, ceramic tiles and Corian have largely superseded these – especially laminates which are hard-wearing, possess variety of pattern and colour and are inexpensive. Ceramic tiles need much more attention to keep them hygienic and clean.

Du Pont Corian is a man-made 'stone' which can be worked like wood and is a solid non-porous material. It is almost impossible to stain, is more heat resistant than conventional worktops, and accidental scratches or knife marks can simply be sandpapered away. Corian's big advantage is that sinks and tops can be designed as one piece, so there are no cracks or crevices to harbour dirt and bacteria or allow water to seep through. Any household cleaning products can be used, so it is easy to care for.

A new development in plastic laminates by Formica, called ColorCore, eliminates the dark edge which always showed where the laminate was cut and joined. The new material is solid colour throughout. This means that nicks and chips in the laminate are less obvious. ColorCore is also claimed to be more wear-resistant than standard laminates.

Sinks and taps

As there are now so many sink combinations on the market, it is unnecessary to go into lengthy explanations. The illustrations overleaf will give you an idea of some of the many types available.

There is nothing worse than a dripping tap. And a tap which leaks from the base causes aggravation. Taps so shaped that they cannot be cleaned around, harbouring dirt and germs, are also annoying as well as dangerous. Handles that need dry hands to turn them on and spouts not long enough or tall enough to enable you to wash up large or elongated items, are equally unsatisfactory. There are mixer taps that splash water because control valves are inaccurate.

The most useful taps are those mixers that are plumbed in to the wall behind the sink. They take up no work surface space and are easily accessible for cleaning. But because the majority of sinks in Britain are fixed under a window, these wall taps are unusable. In those instances where the sink is against a wall, the wall-mounted mixer taps are more practical.

Lever action fittings are normally only used in hospitals or institutions, but they can be even more useful in domestic kitchens when it is some-times very practical to be able to turn on the water with an elbow. New developments in imported taps ensure that far more of them meet National Water Council standards, as well as regulating the water flow within the mixer. Ceramic valves replace old-fashioned washers and internal components are made from materials which will reject hard water deposits.

Taps come in colours to match sinks, hobs and handles but not all conform to water authority specifications, so check before buying. Integral brushes and washing up liquid dispensers are good in theory, but receive little enthusiasm from those who have them in their kitchens.

Waste disposal units

Critics of waste disposal units say they are noisy; that cutlery can be mangled; and that extra food particles in sewers could lead to an increase in the number of rats breeding. If they are badly fitted or supplied with a weak motor they can be more trouble than they are worth. Unclogging blocked drains and untangling string caught around the blades is a major chore. But they are ideal to get rid of scraps of food and smelly waste bins both hygienically and quickly, necessary in many households, especially in flats.

There are two types of disposers. With batch feed disposers, a batch of rubbish is put into the chamber and the plug and cold tap switched on. The grinding chamber is totally enclosed during the grinding operation. Continuous feed dis-posers allow waste to be processed continuously with cold, flowing water, without switching it off to reload. To ensure the food is safely pushed

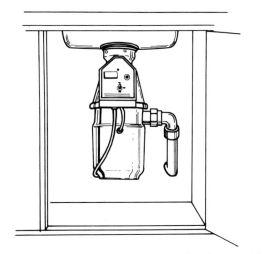 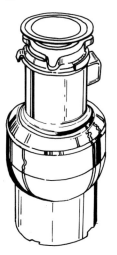 

There are a variety of waste disposal units available.

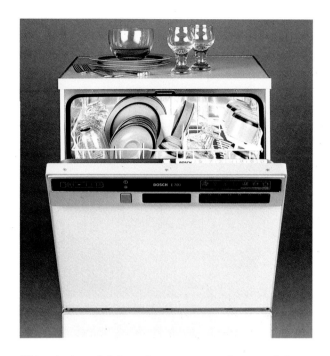

This selection of sinks and taps give an indication of the variety available.

◊ ◊ Brittany ceramic sink and drainer.

◊ ◊ Twin square-bowl sinks in brown enamel.

◊ Sink, small bowl and drainer in stainless steel.

◊ Two-and-a-half bowl sinks in stainless steel.

◊ Wall-mounted lever taps, ideal if your sink is not beneath a window.

◊ Lever-action, surface-mounted taps.

◁ Although the British lag behind America and most of Europe in owning dishwashers, the majority of those who use them would be loath to give them up.

down into the grinding chamber, a wooden spoon may be used. The grinders and impellers at the base of the chamber pulverise the food waste into a fine slurry which is then washed away into the drainage system.

Although coping with most food waste, from experience, electrically-powered disposers do not deal very well with artichoke leaves, banana skins, other soft, stringy vegetables or large meat bones. Chop bones need a lot of noisy grinding before they disappear. Sink waste disposers, of course, will not deal with bottles, tins, paper or plastic which will only gum up the works, ruin the grinders and block the pipes. A ½-hp motor will cope better with waste than a smaller model, and an outer casing will insulate the sound more effectively.

If you plan to install a waste disposer into an existing stainless steel sink, tools are available to cut a 90 mm waste hole. A new sink should have a waste of 90 mm. Always check before you buy in case the unit can't be fitted for some reason, such as not being on mains drainage.

Kitchen units

Units are first and foremost a matter of personal taste. Kitchen unit manufacturers tend to copy each other's designs and use virtually the same interior fitments and fittings to produce fairly similar end products. The occasional manufacturer will use, say, an exclusive dust seal around the doors, or ventilate the larder unit, which may or may not appeal to you.

What is important to someone about to invest in a new kitchen is that the manufacturer, shop or studio has a good reputation. Then should anything go wrong (and it happens even in the best regulated transformations) the problem will be rectified without too many hassles. Beware of the here-today-gone-tomorrow salesman who promises you a dream kitchen which turns into a nightmare once he's taken your money, leaving you no kitchen and no forwarding address!

Ovens and hobs

A kitchen can still function without fitted units, but without a cooker it loses all meaning. Gas or electric? Free-standing, split-level or built-under? Fan, solid fuel, ceramic, microwave, British or Continental? The choice is bewildering.

According to the Electricity Council, the British as a nation grill and bake more frequently and roast meat more often and more slowly than do Continental cooks. Most British housewives therefore find the Continental oven with integral grill inconvenient.

The position of oven controls can be either eye level or waist height. Grills can also be at these levels. Your choice will depend on your height, and your eyesight. Though some of our survey respondents felt it really didn't matter as long as

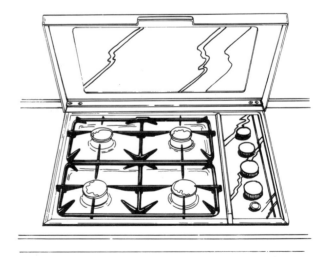

The choice of ovens is bewildering, so take your time when choosing what is right for you.

the grill cooked efficiently. Unless carefully planned within the layout, a split-level cooker can take up too much space in a small room. But the advantages of no bending, ease of cleaning, and extra storage in housing units far outweigh this criticism.

Built-under ovens are a streamlined alternative, but have the disadvantage of the grill inside the oven. It is necessary to bend to remove food from the oven.

With both these combinations you are able to mix your fuels, gas hob with electric oven, or vice versa.

Fan cooking needs some clarification. Fan ovens are more economical as they need no preheating and cooking temperatures are slightly lower. Heat is evenly spread throughout the oven. Cooking time and shrinkage of food are both reduced. Less splashing during cooking

means less cleaning.

A fan-assisted oven circulates the heat evenly around the oven (generally British made), whilst other types direct heat through ducts in individual shelves (Continental method). The gas industry has produced its own version of a gas-fired fan oven, and have advanced a stage further. This fan/gas/microwave combination cooker, also has a self-clean programme. It is certainly a breakthrough in combining technologies and energies.

If your choice is split level, the hob need not be the same make or even the same fuel as the oven. A hob can have two, four, or six plates or burners. It can also incorporate a long, narrow hot plate, a deep fryer, a charcoal grill, or a bain marie. It too can be mixed fuels: two gas, two electric plates or ceramic. Electric plates aren't as instantly responsive as gas, but they are easier to clean. Instantly controllable electric hobs are now becoming available with the use of tungsten halogen filaments. But if you do choose gas you can obtain hermetically sealed burners and a choice of different colours to match sinks.

Pan supports can be a big problem when they chip or stain or even disintegrate. Stainless steel pan supports always mark and this cannot be removed. Make sure that pan supports hold your smallest pan without it tilting onto the burner.

Automatic and spark ignitions on gas hobs sometimes fail after a while and frequently fail if handled incorrectly. Thermostatic 'pan-sensors' are available on some gas and electric models and are useful for control of either high or low temperature cooking.

Ceramic hobs consist of a smooth sheet of ceramic glass that is non porous and durable beneath which are two or four radiant heating elements. On the surface of the ceramic glass there are circular patterned areas to indicate the size and positioning of the heating elements

105

⌂ *The three ovens above give an indication of the range available. Top right, the latest fan gas cooker with a microwave in the oven. At the top, a ceramic hob slip-in cooker with waist level grill and digital controls. Above, a built-in electric oven with hob unit above.*

◊ *The choice of units is vast; the influence is Far Eastern on this manila bamboo kitchen.*

◊ *A built-in fridge with integrated door to match the kitchen units.*

◊ *Microwave ovens can be built in above cookers or fridges to save valuable worktop space.*

beneath the glass. The colours are either white, mottled, brown or black. The darker the surface the easier it is to clean. Some hobs have extra safety features – usually a large neon warning light on the control panel which glows for 20 to 30 minutes after the element has been used to warn that the surface may still be hot.

The depth of most hobs has in the past been too great to allow a drawer or pull-out table or appliance to fit underneath. But many manufacturers are now able to produce a shallow 30 mm deep hob which makes for far greater flexibility.

Fridges, fridge/freezers, freezers

These are today's equivalent of the pantry and larder. These appliances do everything from storing vegetables and dairy products at ready-to-eat temperatures, to deep freezing carcases of meat to be eaten months later. It's an added bonus if they can defrost themselves or produce ice at the push of a lever, and even store all the packets that we buy. Isn't it time, though, that fridges accommodated odd-shaped bottles such as Perrier water – after all that bottle has been in existence for 100 years!

The majority of fridges are simple upright oblong boxes. Sometimes small freezers are fitted inside the cabinet for storing already frozen food and ice cubes. Sometimes there is a separate freezer for freezing fresh produce, or a combination which has a chiller, fridge and freezer. A chiller is a self-contained cool compartment in the fridge which maintains dairy produce at ready-to-eat temperature.

One enlightened manufacturer has produced a combination of chiller, fridge, freezer and compartment that can operate as either freezer or fridge.

Doors can be hinged either left or right, so they can open most efficiently into your kitchen.

Have you ever walked into a kitchen and found yourself unable to spot the fridge? It is finally discovered cunningly concealed inside a unit. This is a built-in model with a unit door attached to the door of the fridge. Or it may be a piece of matching laminate applied to the front of the fridge door. These are called decor panels. To fit inside a housing unit an integrated fridge is somewhat smaller than most and should it go wrong some years later, it is often a major chore to replace it with something of the same dimensions.

It is preferable to keep the freezer out of the kitchen if it is a separate unit, as it will use less electricity in a cooler room. An upright freezer is more expensive to run, needs defrosting more frequently and it is easier to leave the door open accidentally. Unless the interior is very roomy it won't take huge lumps of meat or a large turkey that can be such a bargain. However, for a shorter height person, a chest freezer can be a big mistake. You can lose something forever at the bottom of a chest freezer!

Dishwashers

Only four per cent of British households own a dishwasher. Britain lags way behind Italy, West Germany and America, for example. An average of ten hours per week is spent in washing up by hand, drying and putting away. To stack, unload and store away the contents of a dishwasher only takes ten minutes per day. Tea towels and dishcloths harbour potentially dangerous bacteria which thrive on handwashed plates, even when hot water and powerful detergents are used. Research shows a seven-fold increase of bacteria on handwashed items.

Having given a dishwasher house room, people are loath to give them up. The majority of them are manufactured in West Germany or Italy even though they carry a British brand name. Even if you think you're buying a British

Electronic washing machines are now common.

machine, you probably are not! Even so, the majority conform to high standards of performance and safety. Free-standing or built in, the dishwasher should fit under a standard 600 mm worktop, although sometimes the plumbing will push it proud of the units either side and a 650 mm depth worktop will be needed. Free-standing dishwashers may take a decor panel, but built-ins are designed to have doors and a plinth line to match the kitchen units. A 12-place setting is standard, but the free-standing worktop models take six. However, they can be more expensive than the lower priced 12-place machine.

As rack design varies from one machine to another it is wise to take a selection of your own crockery to the shop to ensure it fits into the dishwasher of your choice.

Except for lead crystal glass, antique china, wooden or bone handled cutlery, everything else can be put into the dishwasher. Unless pans need scouring, they too can benefit.

A programme lasts about 90 minutes. Most machines have a built-in water softener activated by coarse salt, which if not regularly topped up will result in cloudiness and grittiness. A rinse aid adds shine. Cold-fill machines ensure that the contents get extra rinsing while the water heats. A rinse-and-hold programme is useful for rinsing between full loads.

A hot-fill machine is economical if hot water is plentiful. The cycle is shorter, but there is no rinse-and-hold programme.

Washing machines

More than 80 per cent of British households now own a washing machine. Electronic technology added into them has increased the range of programmes and helped to conserve energy.

As fast as synthetic fabrics are being developed, traditional crafts of spinning pure cotton and wool are being revived. The washing machine has to cope with these variations. Research and development has to be done in conjunction with detergent and textile manufacturers. No machine can handle delicate fabrics unless the powder has the right chemical reaction with the temperature of the water used. Comments made in our survey revealed that people were often ignorant of the need for a careful sorting of any machine load and of correct programme choice, yet expected their washing to come out of the machine perfect every time.

Incorporating a micro chip into a washing machine enables it to trace faults in the mechanism and clearly display the sector which has the fault.

Chapter 11

Survey Results

Major decisions about what units and appliances are right for you are tackled in this chapter which highlights the features of kitchen equipment which came in for specific praise or criticism in our survey.Factors to consider when you are choosing equipment include – do you need two sinks or one? What is the advantage of a waste disposal unit? Is an extractor fan better than a charcoal hood? Which oven, dishwasher, washing machine is right for me?

In most cases, the opinion of a friend about their machine is more valuable than relying on a salesman who is often more concerned with making the sale than giving impartial advice – if he is qualified to do so. He cannot know the finer points of a machine if he has not used it. He certainly cannot know the quirks of a dishwasher if his only experience is the occasional help he offers his wife at home when washing dishes by hand. The comments of someone who has actually used the item are bound to be the most informed – and you do need to know if a pair of taps will splash or whether you can operate the tap handles when your hands are wet!

To give you practical and informed answers to these real questions, we conducted a user survey. This revealed what people thought of their equipment and how it performed under domestic conditions. We asked about all types of kitchen equipment from free-standing and split-level cookers to fridges, freezers and tumble dryers.

The results were enlightening – sometimes predictable. There was general disappointment with the overall drop in quality of most domestic appliances. But everyone loved their dishwasher, with only minor criticisms. Waste disposers were either loved – or hated. Extractor units were greatly criticised, as were some built-in ovens. On further investigation, we discovered that people expected far more from their appliance than it was capable of giving. For instance, extractor fans, as they are presently constructed, have to be noisy in operation because of the sound of the motor which draws up the fumes. But, though they cannot extract all odours immediately, they do stop cooking smells lingering.

Advertising for the sort of equipment tackled in the survey (in contrast to advertising for, say, perfume or some other non-functional product) ought to educate and inform. It should be possible for the potential purchaser to find out if the machine actually fits their needs – not merely to read that it is 'the best' cooker or washing machine. Advertisements should inform the reader about the degree of sophistication of their products, about the use of controls and ease of cleaning. It should not be necessary to buy an oven and then find out that you need a technology qualification to operate it!

Unfortunately, advertising is often more

concerned with showing beautiful photographs of superb but unused – and sometimes unusable – kitchens, and the information you really need is tucked away out of sight. Do not be put off. Make sure you know your own needs before you look at the brochures, so that you can assess the products carefully and choose what is right for you.

Based on people's actual experience of using products, these findings should help you to ask the right questions about any equipment you are considering for your kitchen.

Appliance	Features praised	Criticisms made
Free-standing cookers Our survey revealed that the most-loved cooker was the Aga. The majority of cookers were both criticised and praised. *Brands surveyed: Belling, Cannon, Carron, Creda, Electrolux, English Electric, Hotpoint, Leisure, Main, Moffatt, New World, Parkinson Cowan.*	eye-level grill two ovens timer inner glass door good design matching decor reliability	inadequate grill absence of self-clean oven liners difficult to clean failure of automatic timer failure of automatic ignition on gas cookers
Ovens The majority of comments on built-in and built-under ovens were favourable. The Miele brand came out virtually without criticism. *Brands surveyed: AEG, Creda, De Dietrich, Miele, Moffatt, Neff, New World, Tappan, Tricity, Westinghouse, Zanussi.*	drop down oven door dual grill easy-to-use controls readability of controls good design easy to clean fast convenient height good for disabled	size grill inside oven bad finish poor design difficult to clean no self-clean oven facility poor wearability slow oven thermostat failure noisy fan oven unclear instructions
Hobs The most popular hobs were the Creda electric models for cleanability. *Brands surveyed: AEG, Belling, Bosch, Carron, Creda, De Dietrich, Miele, Moffatt, Neff, Scholtes, Tappan, Tricity, Westinghouse.*	easy to clean	pan supports poor quality, difficult to clean and quick to discolour controls difficult to read
Fridges The most popular fridges were the AEG models, generally voted good on all counts. *Brands surveyed: Americana, Electra, Electrolux, Ignis, Indesit, Kelvinator, Lec, Miele, Neff, Phillips, Tricity, UPO, Zanussi.*	large interiors accessible shelves automatic defrost easy to clean reliability	too small poor temperature control poorly designed interiors poor interior fittings (universally criticised) brittle plastic hard to clean self defrost failure/no auto defrost abysmal service faulty doors and door seals

Survey results

Appliance	Features praised	Criticisms made
Fridge/freezers The most popular models were Electrolux and Phillips. *Brands surveyed: Beekay Baucknecht, Electrolux, Hotpoint, Ignis, Lec, Phillips.*	good internal design auto defrost facility efficiency reliability easy removal of water	poor components and interior linings poor temperature control clogging up of self-defrost noisy motors
Freezers The most popular models were again Electrolux and Phillips. *Brands surveyed: Admiral, AEG, Americana, Beekay Baucknecht, Bosch, Electra, Electrolux, Esta, Frigidaire, Hotpoint, Ignis, Indesit, Kelvinator, Lec, Miele, Neff, Nova, Novum, Ocean, Phillips, Total, Tricity, UPO, Zanussi, Zoppas.*	accessible shelves and drawers well designed interior large enough to take bulky items (chest freezer) more convenient in use (upright freezer)	insufficient freezer baskets instructions in German only! brittle plastic doors faulty doors difficult to defrost no auto defrost failure of components bad service
Dishwashers Dishwashers were universally liked and greatly appreciated. Criticisms were not as vehement as on other appliances. *Brands surveyed: AEG, Beekay Baucknecht, Bendix, Bosch, Colston, Frigidaire, Hirondo, Hoover, Hotpoint, Indesit, Lylybet, Miele, Neff, Phillips, Servis, Zanussi.*	labour and time-saving large easy to clean easy to load good after-sales service reliable quiet	badly designed and fitting components poor fitting racks difficult to clean expensive and poor service poor wear in use difficult to see level of rinse aid no salt indicator glassware emerges cloudy too many programmes

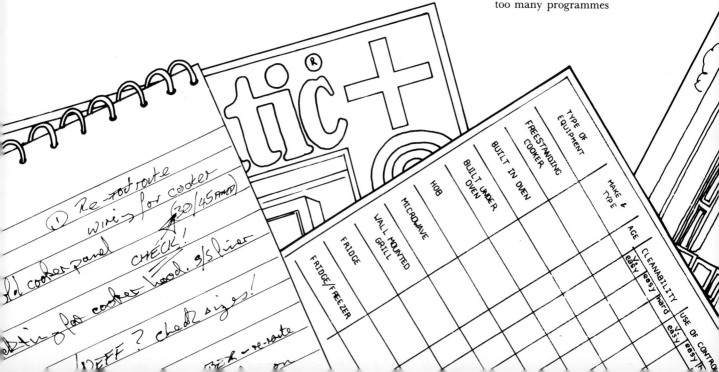

Appliance	Features praised	Criticisms made
Washing machines Most of the people surveyed were satisfied and happy with their washing machines. Basic needs were good results, dependable and efficient machines and good after-sales service. *Brands surveyed: AEG, Bendix, Colston, Creda, Electra, Hoover, Hotpoint, Indesit, Philco Ford, Phillips, Servis, Zanussi.*	good results dependable range of programmes good service labour saving simplicity in use economy button good spin minimal maintenance	poor spin over-complicated instructions insufficient range of programmes too noisy no half-load facility
Tumble dryers A simple piece of domestic equipment, tumble dryers were generally liked, with the AEG model proving the most popular. *Brands surveyed: AEG, Creda, Hoover, Hotpoint, Jackson, Miele, Parnall, Phillips.*	compact easy to clean good controls efficiency low repair costs	noisy in operation expensive to run hard-to-read controls poor wear and design

Sinks
Everyone had definite views about their sinks. The vast majority of those surveyed had stainless steel sinks. The quality of the steel was generally considered inferior to that produced in the past. Corian, ceramic or the Fordham (Asterite) sinks had virtually no criticisms. Enamel and brass sinks were not very popular.
	hygienic
	serviceable
	easy to clean
	large
	coloured enamel: attractive
		insufficiently deeply dished around waste, allowing water to collect around drain holes
		steel: not 'stainless'
		   wore badly
		   scratched easily
		coloured enamel: small
		   easily chipped
		brass: unpopular

Chapter 12

Kitchen of the Future

The typical, labour-saving American dream kitchen that brightened the austere lives of well-to-do families after the second world war, has hardly changed in concept since the 1950s when it was introduced into Britain. At that time it was a quantum leap forward from the 1930s style of labour intensive kitchens, when servants were more plentiful and cheap.

However, since the 1950s people's lives in sophisticated societies have altered dramatically. Bulk buying is more prevalent – freezers, virtually unheard of 30 years ago, are now commonplace – microwave ovens are helping to revolutionise cooking habits, microchips are incorporated into dishwashers and washing machines. Leisure time is expanding and dictating how and when people eat both in and out of the home. These influences indicate the type of food we cook, what we use to cook with, the gadgets and small appliances for speed or economy, and the crockery we need to withstand the rigours of the dishwasher and/or the microwave.

Investment by the kitchen unit manufacturers in capital machinery and plant ensure that the basic carcase construction of units should not be radically altered.

A planned and fully fitted kitchen as we now use the term is a major household expenditure. Besides the expense of buying units and appliances, you may also be paying for an expert planner to design a kitchen that will fit the room,
then an experienced joiner to fit the complicated units into the kitchen and to make sure that every appliance fits its housing unit and works. Plumbers and electricians will also be needed for extending pipe runs and installing a safe wiring system. Should you choose non-standard appliances or if your walls aren't square, the fitter will know just how to overcome these difficulties, without you being aware that there were any. This is what good kitchen fitting is all about and is not something that the consumer is aware of.

Should you wish at a later date to change your built-in oven, or if your integrated fridge malfunctions, you will then realise how difficult it is to alter things. New models supersede the originals and often do not fit the first housing. If you are lucky enough to find an ingenious joiner who can modify the units, it will still cost a good deal in time and money. On the other hand, soon after fitting your kitchen you may have to move house, but you won't be able to take the kitchen with you.

Computers and video cassette recorders are mostly sold for games, entertainment and business uses at the moment. We expect to see them put to more practical use in the kitchen. A flat video screen could display information on stocks of household goods, recipes, cassettes of cookery demonstrations, local community information, and where to obtain the bargain of the week. Controls for heating, lighting and air conditioning would also be within a central control panel in the kitchen.

Because of the delicacy of the equipment, a computer in the kitchen itself is not a practical possibility. Spill a cup of coffee over your keyboard and thousands of pounds of equipment is wrecked. With the speed of technological revolution we assume these mundane problems will be overcome.

Ideally, all electrical appliances should be connected to the household's central computer to be controlled by the family. Faults in any machine can then easily be detected and possibly remedied before they become major.

With increased leisure time the male influence in the home will be greater. Home cooking will become a creative pursuit, rather than simply a way of keeping body and soul together. But if the male of the species is involved, he will not put up with the kitchen being tucked away in the corner of the house. Homes of the future will be built without fixed internal walls. The tendency towards combining kitchen and dining room to form one large living area has been well established and is documented in this book. It now only remains for architects and builders to recognise the needs of the consumer and start building homes for people instead of for the drawing board. The kitchen of the future needs to be both mobile and flexible, in which equipment and siting can be changed when circumstances so demand.

Lateral-thinking designers are currently working on many ideas for future living. John Prizeman and George Fejer, two notable and

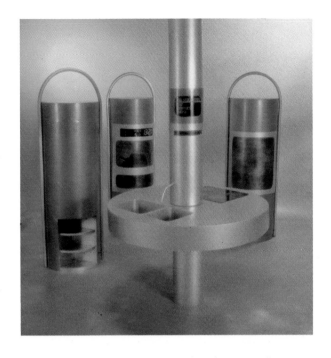

△ *The kitchen of the future is becoming more of a reality as technology advances into the home.*

leading practical designers, have been presenting revolutionary ideas in this field for twenty years, and gradually their concepts are becoming more acceptable as technology catches up with their ideas. Capsule kitchens, mobile work centres, cylinder kitchens, 'touch controlled' kitchens, will all find a place and these concepts are moving nearer and nearer to reality for the majority, rather than being an idealised image for the designer.

Chapter 13

Financing Your Kitchen Improvements

You may need to borrow money for a new kitchen or major improvement to an existing kitchen. In fact, this may be the best plan anyway, by virtue of the tax relief you will gain on the interest you pay on the loan. Home improvements are generally considered a very good loan risk if the dwelling's value is increased at the end of it. Basic sources of funding are listed below.

1. THE BANK: Funds may be obtained by extending your bank mortgage or, if you do not have one, then a personal loan might be possible.
2. THE BUILDING SOCIETY: If you have a mortgage, your Building Society should be prepared to extend it to cover home improvement expenditure, as long as you can prove you are able to meet the increased repayments. Some building societies also operate separate home improvement loan schemes and have literature available on the subject.
3. FINANCE HOUSES: A loan for a new kitchen can be obtained from one of the many reputable finance houses. They often work in conjunction with kitchen showrooms, builders merchants and the Gas and Electricity authorities. For those without a bank account, or without a mortgage, this method of finance may be more suitable, though the interest rates will be higher.
4. NATIONALISED INDUSTRIES: A complete kitchen ordered via the Gas or Electricity Board showroom's kitchen planning service may be financed by credit instalments with one of the finance houses.
5. GRANTS: An improvement grant from the local authority might possibly be relevant if the property fits one of the range of improvement grant categories. The subject is complex, and local council's attitudes are not consistent around the country. Most councils have an improvement grants office and should be able to supply a leaflet on this subject. Your local consumer advice centre of Citizens Advice Bureau may also be able to advise.

If it seems that your property is eligible for one of the categories of home improvement grant, persistence may need to be applied as many local authorities make it extremely difficult for the uninitiated to obtain access to these funds.

Information Sources

Finance

Building Societies Association, 34 Park Street, London W1Y 3PF.

Finance Houses Association, 18 Upper Grosvenor Street, London W1X 9PB.

Department of the Environment (improvement grant leaflets) see Yellow Pages.

Nationalised Industries

British Gas, 326 High Holborn, London WC1.

Electricity Council, 30 Millbank, London SW1P 4RD.

Solid Fuel Advisory Service, National Coal Board, Hobart House, Grosvenor Place, London SW1.

Approved Contractors and Installers

Electrical Contractors Association, 32 Palace Court, London W2.

National Inspection Council for Electrical Installation Contracting, (NICEIC), 93 Albert Embankment, London SE1.

Confederation of Registered Gas Installers, CORGI, St Martin's House, 140 Tottenham Court Road, London W1P 9LN.

Heating & Ventilating Contractors Association, 34 Palace Court, London W2 4JD.

National Association of Plumbing, Heating & Mechanical Services Contractors, 13 Newton Road, Leeds LS7 4DL.

General

Consumers Association, 14 Buckingham Street, London WC2.

British Electrotechnical Approvals Board for Household Equipment (BEAB), Mark House, The Green, 9–11 Queens Road, Hersham, Walton-on-Thames, Surrey KT12 5LU.

Builders Merchants Federation, 15 Soho Square, London, W1.

National Home Improvement Council, 26 Store Street, London WC1E 7BT.

The Building Centre,
26 Store Street, London WC1E 7BT
Colston Avenue, The Centre, Bristol BS1 4TW
Green Lane, Durham DH1 3JY
3/4 Claremont Terrace, Glasgow G3 7PF
113/115 Portland Street, Manchester M1 6FB
The Design Centre, Haymarket, London SW1.

British Tile Council, Federation House, Station Road, Stoke-on-Trent, Staffs.

Index

Index